CONTEMPORARY CHRONICLES
OF THE MIDDLE AGES.

CONTEMPORARY CHRONICLES OF THE MIDDLE AGES.

Sources of twelfth-century history.

From the South of England:

WILLIAM OF MALMESBURY
A history of his own times,
from 1135 to 1142.

From the North of England:

RICHARD OF HEXHAM
The acts of King Stephen and the
Battle of the standard, 1135 to 1139,

and

JORDAN FANTOSME
The war between the English and the
Scots in 1173 and 1174.

Translated from the Latin
By Joseph Stephenson.
Published by
LLANERCH ENTERPRISES,
Felinfach, Dyfed, SA48 8PJ.
1988

4

Contents

Extracts from Stephenson's preface to:

The Hexham historians* 9

Jordan Fantosme 10

William of Malmesbury's own preface 11

William of Malmesbury's
history of his own times 12

Richard of Hexham's history of the
acts of King Stephen and the
Battle of the Standard 53

Jordan Fantosme's history of the
war between the English and the
Scots in 1173 and 1174 77

*Note - there were two Hexham historians, John and Richard. Only the more important work of Richard of Hexham is included.

Malmesbury and Hexham are translated from the Latin, Fantosme from Old French.

Joseph Stephenson's translations were first published by Seeley's of London in the 1850's in a series entitled The Church Historians of England.

ALTHOUGH universal suffrage has assigned the highest rank amongst the English Historians to William of Malmesbury, yet there are few of our writers concerning whose personal history we have such scanty information. The particulars respecting him which have descended to our times, are, for the most part, gleaned from his own writings, and these notices are fragmentary and unimportant. We learn, indeed, from himself, that one of his parents was of Norman descent, the other of English; but as to their names, residence, and position in society, we know nothing. We are equally ignorant as to the time and place of his birth; but if we may venture to adopt a statement advanced by some biographers, we shall rank him among the natives of the county of Somerset. The love of knowledge which was so conspicuous in his later years, exhibited itself at an early period of his life, and he has preserved an account of the occupations and the studies of his boyhood in a passage of sufficient importance to be inserted entire.

"A long period has elapsed since, as well through the care of my parents as by my own industry, I became familiar with books. This pleasure possessed me from my childhood; this source of delight has grown with my years; indeed, I was so instructed by my father, that had I turned aside from these to other pursuits, I should have considered it as jeopardy to my soul, and discredit to my character. Mindful, therefore, of the adage, 'Covet what is necessary,' I constrained my early age to desire eagerly that which it was disgraceful not to desire. I gave, indeed, my attention to various branches of literature, but in different degrees. Logic, for instance, which gives arms to eloquence, I contented myself with barely hearing; medicine, which ministers to the health of the body, I studied with somewhat more of attention; but having scrupulously examined the several branches of ethics, I bow down to its majesty, because it spontaneously unveils itself to those who study it, and directs their minds to moral practice; history more especially, which, by a certain agreeable recapitulation of past events, excites its readers, by example, to frame their lives to the pursuit of good, or to aversion from evil. When, therefore, at my own personal expense, I had procured some historians of foreign nations, I proceeded, during my domestic leisure, to inquire if anything concerning our own country could be found worthy of handing down to posterity. Hence it arose that, not content with the writings of ancient times, I began myself to compose; not, indeed, in order to display my learning, which is comparatively nothing, but to bring to light events lying concealed in the confused mass of antiquity. In consequence, rejecting vague opinions, I have studiously sought for chronicles, far and near, though I confess I have scarcely profited anything by this industry; for, perusing them all, I still remain poor in information, though I carried out my researches as long as I could find anything to read."

The period to which this extract relates,—the period of anarchy which followed upon the Norman invasion, was one which made the seclusion of a cloister the only safe refuge for a youth of such a disposition as that described above : and we need feel no surprise at discovering the future historian of England an inmate of the Benedictine establishment of Malmesbury. Here, while he devoted himself to the discharge of his more immediate duties, he found leisure for the prosecution of his self-imposed studies. These were directed partly to theology, but chiefly to history, general, local, and biographical ; and the list of his writings preserved by Tanner, Cave, and others, evinces the zeal and the industry of his pen.

The " Historia Novella," or as I have ventured to para- phrase the title, " The History of his Own Times," embraces that period of English history which intervened between the death of Henry the First (A.D. 1135) and the year one thousand one hun- dred and forty-two. It ends in a manner somewhat abrupt, which leads to the inference that it does not fully represent the latest intentions of the author, and that a more extended narrative was in contemplation, if not in active progress, when his labours were interrupted by death ; and at the same time the variations which occur in the different copies—variations which have evidently pro- ceeded from the hand of the author —prove that upon this portion of his work, also, Malmesbury's busy pen was employed, until the latest moment, in minute alterations and corrections.

Malmesbury was sufficiently well acquainted with the remains of classical antiquity to understand the distinction between a chronicle and a history ; and he aimed at the production of a work which should be honoured with the latter designation. This ambition has been attended with results which we cannot but regret, for it has induced him to pass by, as trivial and undignified, many circumstances, to us of exceeding value, and with which he must have been acquainted ; circumstances which probably would have found a place in the pages of the less aspiring chronicler. More than this, his proposed imitation of classical antiquity has too often given an artificial and constrained tone to his narrative of events which occurred within the range of his own observation. We have to lament—what was to him a cause of self-gratulation—that he has so liberally " seasoned his crude materials with Roman salt." What between his theory and his mode of working it out, we are too often defrauded of information with which we should have been thankful to have been made acquainted, and the result is frequently disappointment and regret.

All this, however, is said without the remotest wish to detract from the acknowledged merits of our author as an historian. Taking him at his own stand-point, and judging of his work accord- ing to his own abstract estimate of perfection, we cannot but assign to it a high grade of intrinsic excellence. He is cautious how he accepts evidence, calm in the judgment which he pro- nounces upon disputed questions, and dispassionate when he arbi- trates between conflicting interests.

Two priors of the Augustinian priory of St. Andrew's, of Hexham, in the county of Northumberland, have written continuations of the chronicle of Simeon of Durham.

"The History of the Church of Hexham, by John the prior," embraces a period of twenty-five years, namely, from A.D. 1130 to 1154, both inclusive.

Of greater value is the "History of the Acts of king Stephen, and the Battle of the Standard," by Richard, prior of Hexham. It extends from A.D. 1135 to 1139, both inclusive; and is occupied chiefly with an account of the irruptions of the Scots, under king David, into the northern districts of England, of which it gives some painful details. Its Hexham origin is frequently perceptible (pp. 43, 44, 52), and the information which it affords is valuable, as the contemporaneous narrative of a well-informed historian.

A translation of the curious metrical "Chronicle of Jordan Fantosme" next claims the reader's notice. It gives a detailed account of the war carried on by William the Lion, king of Scotland, against Henry the second, king of England, which terminated in the capture of the former, near Alnwick, in Northumberland.

The author, Jordan Fantosme, who frequently mentions himself in the course of his poem (see lines 521, 668, 674, 903, and 1152), was undoubtedly well acquainted with many of the circumstances which he has recorded. Thus (at lines 445—449) he states that he was an eye-witness of the atrocities perpetrated at Wark by the Scottish invaders. At line 1731, he speaks of his information "of his own knowledge." He was undoubtedly present at the capture of the Scottish king, for in his minute description of that event he takes care to say (line 1774): "I do not relate a fable, as one who has heard say, but as one who was there, and I myself saw it. And again we have his statement, "with my two eyes I saw it," (line 1810.) In contrast with this, he tells us that his account of the siege and capture of Norwich was not derived from personal observation (line 896); and, on another occasion, he thus addresses his readers (line 1910), "As far as I know, now hear the truth."

In the midst, however, of this minute personal acquaintance with his subject, we are struck by observing that he commits the singular geographical blunder of supposing that the town of Berwick stands upon the river Tyne (lines 428, 1186), a mistake which would seem to imply that he was not a native of, and had not been long a resident in these districts.

The external information which we possess respecting a Jordan Fantosme(doubtless the author of the present poem) helps us to a solution of a portion of this difficulty. We learn from some proceedings in a lawsuit, respecting lands in Hampshire, that in A.D. 1160, "magister Jordanus Fantasma" was in the service of Henry de Blois, bishop of Winchester, and brother of king Stephen; and it further appears, from a letter addressed to pope Adrian by John of Salisbury, that he was engaged in a dispute with a clerk named John Joichel, who, without the permission of Fantasma, had opened a school at Winchester. Hence we can understand how a foreigner, probably a Norman by birth, and a resident of Winchester, should be at fault in his nomenclature of the localities of Northumberland.

Two manuscripts of this poem are known to be extant, one in the library of the dean and chapter of Durham, the other in that of the dean and chapter of Lincoln. Both these copies are of the thirteenth century, and they agree very closely together, each scribe affording us the means of correcting the errors and supplying the omissions of the other.

WILLIAM OF MALMESBURY

PREFACE TO THE HISTORY OF HIS OWN TIMES.

Addressed to Robert, Earl of Gloucester.

To his most loving lord, Robert, son of king Henry, and earl of Gloucester, William, the Librarian of Malmesbury, wishes, after completing his victorious course on earth, eternal triumph in heaven. Many of the transactions of your father, of glorious memory, I have not omitted to record, both in the fifth book of my Regal History, and in those three smaller volumes, which I have intituled Chronicles.[2] Your highness is now desirous that those events which, through the miraculous power of God, have taken place in recent times, in England, should be transmitted to posterity; truly, like all your other desires, a most noble one. For what more concerns the advancement of virtue, what more conduces to justice, than to recognise the Divine favour towards good men, and his vengeance upon the wicked? What, too, more grateful, than to commit to the page of history the exploits of brave men, by whose example others may shake off their indolence, and take up arms in defence of their country? As this task is committed to my pen, I think the narrative will proceed with exacter order, if, going back a little, I trace the series of years from the return of the empress into England, after the death of her husband. First, therefore, invoking the help of God, as is fitting, and purposing to write the truth, without listening to enmity, or sacrificing to favour, I shall begin as follows.

---

[1] Terentii Andria, i. 1.
[2] What these were is unknown, as it is believed that there is no MS. of them now to be met with.

WILLIAM OF MALMESBURY'S HISTORY OF HIS OWN TIMES.

BOOK I.

§ 1. IN the twenty-sixth year of Henry king of England, which was in the year of our Lord one thousand one hundred and twenty-six, Henry emperor of Germany, to whom Matilda, the aforesaid king's daughter, had been married, died[1] in the very bloom of his life and of his conquests. Our king was, at that time, residing in Normandy, to quell whatever tumults might arise in those parts. As soon as he heard of the death of his son-in-law, he recalled his daughter, by honourable messengers despatched for that purpose. The empress, as they say, returned with reluctance, as she had become habituated to the country which was her dowry, and had large possessions there. It is well known, that several princes of Lorrain and Lombardy came, during succeeding years, repeatedly into England, to ask her in marriage; but they lost the fruit of their labours, the king designing by the marriage of his daughter, to procure peace between himself and the earl of Anjou. He was certainly, in an extraordinary degree, the greatest of all kings in the memory either of ourselves, or of our fathers : and yet, nevertheless, he ever, in some measure, dreaded the power of the earls of Anjou. Hence it arose, that he broke off and annulled the espousals[2] which William, his nephew, afterwards earl of Flanders, was said to be about to contract with the daughter of Fulk, earl of Anjou, who was afterwards king of Jerusalem. Hence, too, it arose, that he united a daughter of the same earl to his son William, while yet a stripling; and hence it was, that he married his daughter (of whom we began to speak), after her imperial match, to a son of the same Fulk, as my ensuing narrative will show.

§ 2. In the twenty-seventh year of his reign, in the month of September, king Henry came to England, bringing his daughter with him. But, at the ensuing Christmas, convening a great number of the clergy and nobility at London, he gave the county of Salop to his wife, the daughter of the earl of Louvain, whom he had married after the death of Matilda. Distressed that this lady had no issue, and fearing lest she should be perpetually childless, with well-founded anxiety, he turned his thoughts on a successor to the kingdom. On which subject, having held much previous and long-continued deliberation, he now at this council compelled all the nobility of England, as well as the bishops and abbots, to make oath, that, if he should die without male issue, they would, without delay or hesitation, accept his daughter Matilda, the late empress, as their sovereign; observing, how prejudicially to the country, fate

---

[1] The emperor Henry V. died 23d of May A. D. 1125; and in Sept. 1126, king Henry returned from Normandy with his daughter, the empress.
[2] See History of the Kings, § 419.

had snatched away his son William, to whom the kingdom by right had pertained; and that his daughter still survived, to whom alone the legitimate succession belonged, from her grandfather, uncle, and father, who were kings, as well as from her maternal descent for many ages back: inasmuch as from Egbert, king of the West Saxons, who first subdued or expelled the other kings of the island, in the year of the Incarnation eight hundred, through a line of fourteen kings, down to the year one thousand and forty-three, in which king Edward, who lies at Westminster, was elevated to the throne, the line of royal blood did never fail nor falter in the succession.[1] Moreover, Edward, the last, and at the same time the most noble of that stock, had united[2] Margaret, his grand-niece by his brother Edmund Ironside, to Malcolm king of Scotland, whose daughter Matilda, as was well known, was the empress's mother.

§ 3. All, therefore, in this council, who were considered as persons of any note, took the oath: and first of all, William, archbishop of Canterbury; next, the other bishops, and the abbots in like manner. The first of the laity who swore was David, king of Scotland, uncle of the empress; then Stephen, earl of Moriton and Boulogne, nephew of king Henry by his sister Adala; then Robert, the king's son, who was born to him before he came to the throne, and whom he had created earl of Gloucester, bestowing[3] on him in marriage Mabel, a noble and excellent woman; a lady as devoted to her husband as blessed in a numerous and beautiful offspring. There was a singular dispute, as they relate, between Robert and Stephen, contending, with laudable emulation, which of them should take the oath first; one alleging the privilege of a son, the other the dignity of a nephew. Thus all being bound by fealty and by oath, they, at that time, departed to their homes. But after Pentecost, the king sent his daughter into Normandy, ordering her to be betrothed, by the archbishop of Rouen, to the son of Fulk aforesaid, a youth of high nobility and noted courage; nor did he himself delay setting sail for Normandy, for the purpose of uniting them in wedlock. Which being completed, all declared prophetically, as it were, that, after his death, they would break their plighted oath. I have frequently heard Roger bishop of Salisbury say, that he was freed from the oath he had taken to the empress; for that he had sworn conditionally, that the king should not marry his daughter to any one out of the kingdom, without his consent and that of the rest of the nobility: that none of them advised the match, or indeed knew of it, except Robert earl of Gloucester, Brian the earl's son, and the bishop of Lisieux. Nor do I relate this merely because I believe the assertion of a man who knew how to accommodate himself to every change of time and fortune; but, as an historian of veracity, I write the general belief of the people.

§ 4. The remaining years of the life and reign of Henry, I must review briefly, in order that posterity may neither be defrauded of

---

[1] This must be understood with the exception of Cnut and his sons, between Edmund Ironside and Edward the Confessor.

[2] Here seems a mistake. Margaret was given to Malcolm by her brother Edgar Atheling, while in exile in Scotland, A.D. 1067. See Saxon Chronicle.

[3] MSS. E. inserts from "bestowing" to "offspring."

a knowledge of these events; nor that I may seem to dwell on topics little relevant to this history.   In his twenty-eighth year the king returned from Normandy; in his twenty-ninth a circumstance occurred in England which may seem surprising to our long-haired gallants, who, forgetting what they were born, transform themselves into the fashion of females, by the length of their locks.   A certain English knight, who prided himself on the luxuriance of his tresses, being stung by conscience on the subject, seemed to feel, in a dream, as though some person strangled him with his ringlets. Awaking in a fright, he immediately cut off all his superfluous hair. The example spread throughout England, and, as recent punishment is apt to affect the mind, almost all military men allowed their hair to be. cropped in a proper manner without reluctance. But this decency was not of long continuance, for scarcely had a year expired, ere all who thought themselves courtly, relapsed into their former vice; they vied with women in length of locks, and wherever they were defective, put on false tresses, forgetful, or rather ignorant, of the saying of the apostle, "If a man nurture his hair, it is a shame to him."   [1 Cor. xi. 14.][1]   In his thirtieth year [A. D. 1130], king Henry went into Normandy.   Pope Honorius dying in this year, the church of Rome was agitated by great contentions about electing his successor.   There were, at that time, in the city, two very celebrated cardinals, Gregory, deacon of St. Angelo, and Peter, cardinal-priest, son of Leo, prince of the Romans, both noted for learning and activity, nor could the people easily discern which of them more justly ought to be elected by the clergy.   The party, however, which favoured Gregory took the lead, and ordaining him pope, called him Innocent.   Moreover a rumour was disseminated among the people, that Honorius was still just alive, and had commanded this to be done.   The promoters of this choice were, William, bishop of Preneste, Matthew of Albano, Conrad of Sabina, John of Ostia, Peter of Crema, cardinal of St. Chrysogonus, and Haimeric the chancellor.   But the other party, after Honorius was buried, at the instigation of Peter's brothers, who were the most opulent and powerful of the Romans, having elected and consecrated him, gave him the name of Anaclet.   The chief adviser and instigator to this ordination, was Peter, bishop of Portus, whose letter, if I subjoin it, will disclose the whole controversy, although it incline rather to Anaclet.

§ 5.   "Peter, bishop of Portus, to the four bishops, William of Preneste, Matthew of Albano, Conrad of Sabina, and John of Ostia.   How great is the tribulation of my heart for you, He only knows who knows all things; indeed you would have already been acquainted with it, in part, by my letters, did not the sentence and the common authority of the church prohibit.   Of the praise or

---

[1] It is very remarkable what excessive pains were employed to prevail on the young men to part with their locks. In the council held at London by archbishop Anselm, A. D. 1102, it is enacted, that those who had long hair should be cropped, so as to show part of the ear, and the eyes. From the apparently strange manner in which this fashion is coupled in Edmer, p. 81, one might be led to suspect it was something more than mere spleen which caused this enactment. See also Orderic. Vitalis

dispraise of those persons, concerning whom so many different
opinions are at present given, it is not of this world to judge:
there is One who may seek and judge.   But if any be ready to
accuse, one will be ready, and who is also bound to reply; more
especially when both in your and my sight, and in that of the
whole church, each of them has lived discreetly and honestly, and
has hitherto executed his office impartially.   It rather concerns you
to abstain from idle language and the words of haste; if the
question be of report, the business is far different from what your
letters to me declare.   In addition to this; if you regard the
accounts you have published, and the order of proceeding, (with
due reverence to you be it spoken,) by what boldness, by what
assurance, do you presume to call that usurpation of yours an
election?   Why do you call that man of yours ordained, when
there was no order whatever in his case?   Is it thus that you have
learnt to elect a pope?   In a corner, in an hidden place, in darkness, and in the shadow of death?   If you were desirous that a
living should succeed to a dead pope, why would you give out that
the deceased was still alive?   It were much better, surely, to pay
the last sad offices to the dead, and in this manner provide for the
succour of the living; but, behold, while you seek succour for the
living from the dead, you destroy both the living and the dead at
the same time.   Lastly, it was neither your office nor mine to
elect; but rather to refuse or to approve the person elected by the
brethren.   Since, therefore, in neglect of the ritual, contempt of
the canon, and disregard of the very anathema framed by your-
selves, without consulting me your superior, or your elder brethren
and superiors, or even summoning or waiting for them; when you
were inexperienced, and but very few in number, you have pre-
sumed to do this; you must be sensible, from your own estimation
of the case, that it must be considered void and of no avail whatever.   The Lord, however, quickly came to our assistance, and
pointed out a method whereby to obviate your error: for your
brethren the cardinals, (who possess the chief voice in elections,)
together with the whole clergy, at the request of the people, and
with the consent of the nobility, openly, in the light of day, have
unanimously and heartily elected the noble cardinal Peter, as
Roman pontiff, by the name of Anaclet.   I was present at this
election, which was made according to the canons, and have confirmed it by the authority of God.   The church accepts and vene-
rates him, and by the grace of God the bishops and abbots, chief
princes and barons, some by themselves and others by their dele-
gates, acknowledge him in our presence.   The robbery and cruelty
you mention I do not perceive: whoever goes to him for consulta-
tion, or on business, is kindly received, and still more kindly dis-
missed.   Return then, return to your understanding; do not
make a schism in the church; do not persist in this perdition of
souls; let the fear of God possess you, not worldly shame.   Does
any sleep, will he not add that he must rise again?   Cease now
from lies, in which the wicked put their hope.   The lord Tiburtius
hath testified by oath in writing, that I have deemed the deacon of

St. Angelo the only fit person for the office of pope ; let him look
to what he hath said ; I have spoken nothing in secret ; no person
hath ever heard such a word as this from my mouth.   My opinion
always was, that till the pope was buried no mention should be
made of his successor.   I have held, and will hold, the unity of the
church ; I will be careful to adhere to truth and justice, con-
fidently hoping that truth and justice will set me free." After this
manner wrote the aforesaid Peter, bishop of Porto, rather partial
to Peter the son of Leo.   Nor did the other party at all give way;
but called Peter himself, a lion's whelp,[1] and his partisans, the
leaders of a faction.   And they, indeed, acted variously among
themselves under these doubtful circumstances.   Innocent, however, excluded from Rome, passed the Alps and went into France.
Here he was immediately received by all the Cisalpine churches ;
and moreover, even king Henry, who did not easily change his
opinion, willingly acknowledged him at Chartres ; and at Rouen
condescended to honour him, not only with presents from himself,
but also from the nobility, and even the Jews.   Yet Innocent,
though greatly assisted by the kings of England and France, and
the emperor of Germany, could never enjoy peace, because Anaclet
occupied the see of Rome.   However, Anaclet himself dying in
the eighth year of his usurped papacy, as it was called, Innocent
enjoys the papal dignity unmolested to the present time.[2]

§ 6. [A.D. 1131.] In the thirty-first year of his reign, king Henry
returned to England.   The empress, too, in the same year, arrived
on her native soil, and a full meeting of the nobility being held
at Northampton, the oath of fidelity to her was renewed by such
as had already sworn, and also taken by such as hitherto had not.
In the same year, Louis, king of France, growing aged and
unwieldy through extreme corpulency, commanded his son to be
crowned as successor to the kingdom ; but being killed soon after
by the fall of his horse, Louis caused another of his sons to be
consecrated king, by the hands of the Roman pontiff.   He, they
say, does not degenerate from the ancient valour of the French, and
has also acquired Aquitain as the marriage portion of his wife, which,
it is well known, the kings of France have never held in their own
right, since Louis, son of Charles the Great.

§ 7. [A. D. 1132.]   In the thirty-first[3] year of king Henry, a dreadful murrain among domestic animals extended over the whole of
England: entire herds of swine suddenly perished ; whole stalls of
oxen were swept off in a moment ; the same contagion continued
in the following years, so that no village throughout the kingdom
was free from this calamity, or able to exult at the losses of its
neighbours.   At this time, too, the contention between Bernard,
bishop of St. David's, and Urban of Llandaff, on the rights of their
dioceses, which Urban had illegally usurped, was finally put to rest.
For after being agitated by so many appeals to the court of Rome,

---

[1] An allusion to his name, which signifies a lion.
[2] Pope Innocent died 24 Sept. A.D. 1143.
[3] So both printed copy and the MSS. which have been consulted; but it should
be 1132.

so many expensive journeys, so many debates of lawyers for a
number of years, it was at last terminated, or rather cut short, by
the death of Urban at Rome; the pope also, weighing the equity of
the case, did justice to the piety and right of the bishop of St. David's
by a suitable judgment.   In the same year, William archbishop
of Canterbury personally obtained the legation of England through
the indulgence of the see of Rome.

§ 8. The day before the thirty-second[1] year of his reign was completed, Henry, on the nones of August, (the very day on which he
had formerly been crowned at Westminster,) set sail for Normandy.
This was the last, the fatal voyage of his reign.   The providence of
God, at that time, bore reference in a wonderful manner to human
affairs; for instance, that he should embark, never to return alive,
on that day on which he had originally been crowned so long and
prosperously to reign.   It was then, as I have said, the nones of
August; and on the fourth day of the week,[2] the elements mani-
fested their sorrow at this great man's last departure.   For the sun
on that day, at the sixth hour, shrouded his glorious face, as the
poets say, in hideous darkness, agitating the hearts of men by an
eclipse; and on the sixth day of the week, early in the morning,
there was so great an earthquake that the ground appeared absolutely to sink down, a horrid sound being first heard from beneath
the surface.   During the eclipse I saw stars around the sun; and,
at the time of the earthquake the wall of the house in which I was
sitting was lifted up by two shocks, and settled again with a third.
The king, therefore, continued in Normandy for the space of three[3]
whole years, and so much longer as from the nones of August, on
which day, as has been said, he crossed the sea, to the kalends of
December, on which night he died.   Doubtless, he performed
many things worthy of record while in Normandy, but it was my
design to omit whatever did not come authenticated to my knowledge.   Divers expectations of his return to England were all frustrated by some adverse fate, or by the will of God.   He reigned,
then, thirty-five years, and from the nones of August to the kalends
of December, that is, four months wanting four days.   Engaged in
hunting at Liuns, he was taken suddenly ill.   His malady increasing,
he summoned to him Hugh, whom, from prior of Lewes, he had
made abbot of Reading, and afterwards archbishop of Rouen, who
was justly indebted to him and his heirs for such great favours.
The report of his sickness quickly gathered the nobility around him.
Robert, too, his son, the earl of Gloucester, was present, who, from
his unblemished fidelity and matchless virtue, has deserved to be
especially signalized throughout all ages.   Being interrogated by
these persons as to his successor, he awarded all his territories, on
either side of the sea, to his daughter, in legitimate and perpetual

[1] Malmesbury seems to have committed two oversights here. Henry went to
Normandy for the last time on the third of the nones of August (that is, third,
instead of fifth) A. D. 1133. This is evident from the eclipse he mentions, which
took place on that day, as well as from the testimony of the continuator of Florence
of Worcester, a contemporary writer.
[2] Wednesday, 2d August, 1133.
[3] From what has been said above this should be two.

succession, being somewhat displeased with her husband, as he had
irritated him both by threats and by certain injuries. Having passed
the seventh day of his sickness, he died about midnight. I waive
describing his magnanimous character in this place, as I have been
diffuse upon it in the fifth book of my Regal History. In how
Christian a manner he departed, the following epistle of the aforesaid archbishop of Rouen will testify.

§ 9. "To his Lord and Father, pope Innocent, his servant,
Hugh, priest of Rouen, sends his humble duty. I have deemed it
proper, to write to your fatherly affection concerning the king my
master, never to be remembered but with grief; for, being seized
with sudden sickness, he wished for me to console his sufferings,
and sent messengers as soon as possible for that purpose. I went
and passed three melancholy days with him. Agreeably to my
suggestion, he confessed his sins, he beat his breast, and he laid
aside all his animosities. Through the grace of God, and through
our advice and that of the bishops, he promised to attend to the
amendment of his life. Under this promise, according to our
office, on the third day, and three days successively, we gave him
absolution. He devoutly adored the cross of our Lord, and received his Body and Blood; bestowed his alms thus, saying, ' Let
my debts be paid, let the wages[1] and stipends which I owe be discharged, let the remainder be distributed to the poor. I wish they
who held and do hold his treasures had done thus. At last, I
earnestly stated to him our duty concerning the unction of the
sick, which the church adopted from the apostle St. James; and, at
his own devout request, I anointed him with holy oil. Thus he
rested in peace, and may God grant him the peace he loved."

§ 10. These circumstances relating to the faith of king Henry
when dying, were truly attested by the aforesaid archbishop of
Rouen. The body, royally attended, and borne by the nobility in
turn, was brought to Rouen, where, in a certain retired part of the
principal church, it was disembowelled, lest, becoming putrid, it
should offend the senses of those who approached it. The intes-
tines were buried in the monastery of St. Mary des Prees, near the
city, which, as I hear, he had honoured with no mean presents, as
it had been begun by his mother. His body was kept at Caen till
the season, which was then very boisterous, became more tranquil.

§ 11. In the meantime, Stephen, earl of Mortain and Boulogne,
nephew of king Henry (as I have before said) who, after the king
of Scotland, was the first layman that had sworn fidelity to the
empress, hastened his return into England by way of Whitsand.
The empress, from certain causes, as well as her brother, Robert
earl of Gloucester, and almost all the nobility, delayed returning to
the kingdom. However, some castles in Normandy, the principal
of which was Danfront, espoused the party of the heiress. Moreover, it is well known, that on the day on which Stephen disem-

---

[1] "Liberationes," signifies, sometimes, what we now call liveries, that is, garments; sometimes money at stated periods, or, as we should say, wages: it is
here rendered in the latter sense, as being distinct from "solidatæ," pay or
stipends. Perhaps it was intended to distinguish two orders of persons by this
bequest; servants and soldiers: otherwise it may mean garments and wages.

barked in England, there was, very early in the morning, contrary to the nature of winter in these countries, a terrible peal of thunder, with most dreadful lightning, so that the world seemed well-nigh about to be dissolved. After being acknowledged as king by the people of London and of Winchester, he gained over also Roger bishop of Salisbury, and William de Pont de l'Arche, the keepers of the royal treasures. Yet, not to conceal the truth from posterity, all his attempts would have been vain, had not his brother, Henry bishop of Winchester, who is now legate of the papal see in England, granted him his entire support; allured, indeed, by the fullest expectation that Stephen would follow the example of his grandfather William in the management of the kingdom, and more especially in the strictness of ecclesiastical discipline. In consequence, when Stephen was bound by the rigorous oath which William archbishop of Canterbury required from him, concerning restoring and preserving the liberty of the church, the bishop of Winchester became his pledge and surety. The written tenor of this oath I shall be careful hereafter to insert in its proper place.

§ 12. Stephen, therefore, was crowned king of England on Sunday, the eleventh of the kalends of January [Dec. 22], the twenty-second day after the decease of his uncle, in the year of our Lord's incarnation, one thousand one hundred and thirty-five; in the presence of three bishops, that is, the archbishop, and those of Winchester and Salisbury; but there were no abbots and scarcely any of the nobility. He was a man of activity, but imprudent; strenuous in war; of great mind in attempting works of difficulty; · mild and compassionate to his enemies, and affable to all; kind as far as promise went, but sure to disappoint in its truth and execution: whence he soon afterwards neglected the advice of his brother, befriended by whose assistance, as I have said, he had supplanted his adversaries and obtained the kingdom.

§ 13. In the year of our Lord one thousand one hundred and thirty-six, the wind being now favourable, the body of king Henry was, immediately after Christmas, put on ship-board, and brought to England; and, in the presence of his successor in the kingdom, was buried at the monastery of Reading, which he had liberally endowed, and filled with an order of monks of singular piety. Shortly afterwards, a little before Lent, king Stephen went into Northumberland, that he might have a conference with David, king of Scotland, who was said to entertain hostile sentiments towards him. From David he readily obtained what he wished, because, being softened by the natural gentleness of his manners, or by the approach of old age, he willingly embraced the tranquillity of peace, real or pretended.

§ 14. In the same year, after Easter, Robert earl of Gloucester, of whose prudence Stephen chiefly stood in awe, came to England. While he was yet resident in Normandy, he had most earnestly considered what line of conduct he should determine upon in the present state of affairs. If he became subject to Stephen, it seemed contrary to the oath he had sworn to his sister; if he opposed him, he saw that such conduct could nothing benefit her or his nephews, but would certainly most grievously injure himself. For the king, as I said before, had an immense treasure, which his uncle had been accumulating for many years. His coin, and that of the best quality,[1] was estimated at an hundred thousand pounds; besides which there were vessels of gold and silver, of great weight and inestimable value, collected by the magnificence of preceding kings, and chiefly by Henry.[2] A man possessed of such boundless treasures could not want supporters, more especially as he was profuse, and, what by no means becomes a prince, even prodigal. Soldiers of all kinds, and light-armed troops, were flocking to him, chiefly from Flanders and Brittany. These were a most rapacious and violent race of men; who made no scruple to violate churchyards[3] or rob a church: moreover, not only would they drag men of religious order from their horses, but also make them captive; and this was done not merely by foreigners, but even by the native soldiers, who had abhorred the tranquillity of king Henry's time, because it subjected them to a life of poverty. All these most readily resorted to the prince whom they could easily incline to their purposes, pushing their fortune at the expense of the people. Stephen, indeed, before he came to the throne, from his complacency of manners, and readiness to joke, and sit, and regale, even with low people, had gained so much on their affections as is hardly to be conceived; and already had all the nobility of England willingly acknowledged him. This most prudent earl, therefore, was extremely desirous to convince them of their misconduct, and recal them to wiser sentiments by his presence; for, to oppose Stephen's power, he was unable, from the causes aforesaid: indeed, he had not the liberty of coming to England, unless, appearing as a partaker of their revolt, he dissembled for a time his secret intentions. He did homage to the king, therefore, under a certain condition; namely, so long as he should preserve his rank entire, and maintain his engagements to him; for having long since scrutinized Stephen's disposition, he foresaw the instability of his faith.

§ 15. In the same year, soon after the earl's arrival, the bishops swore fidelity to the king, so long as he should maintain the liberty of the church and the vigour of its discipline. He himself also swore according to the tenor of the following instrument:—

"I, Stephen, by the grace of God, elected king of England by the consent of the clergy and of the people, and consecrated by the lord William, archbishop of Canterbury and legate of the holy Roman church, and afterwards confirmed by Innocent, pope of the holy Roman see, through respect and love towards God, do grant the holy church to be free, and confirm to it all due reverence. I pro-

---

[1] There was a great difference in the money of this period: it was often so debased, that payments were made by weight, or by assay, and not by tale.

[2] The progress of some of Henry's treasure is curious. Theobald, earl of Blois, gave many jewels, which had been bestowed on him by Stephen his brother, to certain abbeys, and these again sold them for four hundred pounds to Suger, abbot of St. Denis. Henry, Suger observes, used to have them set in most magnificent drinking vessels. Suger, ap. Duchesne, iv. 345.

[3] Church-yards were, by the canons, privileged, so that persons in turbulent times conveyed their property thither for security.

mise that I will neither do anything simoniacally, nor permit it to be done, in the church, or in matters ecclesiastical. The jurisdiction and power over beneficed clergy, and over all persons in orders, and their property, and the distribution of effects of ecclesiastics, I admit to be in the hands of the bishops, and confirm it so to be. I grant and appoint, that the immunities of the churches, confirmed by their charters, and their customs observed from ancient usage, do remain inviolate. All the possessions of the churches, and the tenures which they held at the death of my grandfather king William, I grant to them free, and discharged from the claim of all parties : but if the church shall hereafter claim anything as held or possessed before the death of the king, of which it is now deprived, I reserve such matter for discussion, or restitution at my will and pleasure. Moreover, whatever, since that king's death, has been obtained by the liberality of kings, or the gift of princes ; by offerings, or purchase, or by any exchange of the faithful, I confirm. I pledge myself to keep peace, and do justice to all, and to preserve them to my utmost ability. I reserve to myself the forests which king William, my grandfather, and William the Second, my uncle, have made and possessed : all the rest which king Henry added, I give and grant, without molestation, to the churches and the kingdom. And if any bishop or abbot, or other ecclesiastical person, shall have properly distributed[1] his property before his death, or appointed such distribution, I allow it to remain good ; but if he shall have been suddenly seized by death, before making a disposition, let the said distribution be made, at the discretion of the church, for the repose of his soul. Moreover, when the sees shall be vacant, let both them and their whole possessions be committed into the hands and custody of the clergy, or of lawful men of the same church, until a pastor be canonically appointed. I entirely do away all exactions, mischeningas,[2] and injustices, whether illegally introduced by the sheriffs, or any one else. I will observe the good and ancient laws and just customs, in murders, pleas, and other causes, and I command and appoint them to be so observed. Done at Oxford, in the year of our Lord, one thousand one hundred and thirty-six, in the first year of my reign."

§ 16. The names of the witnesses, who were numerous, I disdain to particularise, because he as basely perverted almost everything, as if he had sworn only that he might manifest himself a violator of his oath to the whole kingdom. This easy man must pardon me for speaking the truth ; who, had he entered on the sovereignty lawfully, and not given a ready ear to the insinuations of the malevolent in the administration of it, would have wanted little in any

---

[1] It had been the practice to seize, to the king's use, whatever property ecclesiastics left behind them. Henry Huntingdon relates, that on the death of Gilbert Universalis, bishop of London, who was remarkable for his avarice, all his effects, and among the rest, his boots crammed with gold and silver, were conveyed to the Exchequer. Anglia Sacra, ii. 698. Sometimes, even what has been distributed on a death-bed, was reclaimed for the king. Vide G. Neub. iii. 5.

[2] It seems to have been a vexatious fine imposed on litigants when, in their pleadings, they varied from their declaration.—Murder is sometimes taken in its present acceptation ; sometimes it means a certain fine levied on the inhabitants where murder had been committed.

princely quality. Under him, therefore, the treasures of several churches were pillaged, and their landed possessions given to laymen; the churches of the clergy were sold to foreigners; the bishops made captive, or forced to alienate their property; the abbeys given to improper persons, either through the influence of friendship or for the discharge of debts. Still I think such transactions are not so much to be ascribed to him as to his advisers, who persuaded him that he ought never to want money so long as the monasteries were stored with treasure.

§ 17. [A.D. 1137.] In the year of our Lord one thousand one hundred and thirty-seven, in the beginning of Lent, the king crossed the sea. The earl, too, having thoroughly sounded, and discovered the inclinations of such as he knew to be tenacious of their plighted oath, and arranged what he conceived proper to be done afterwards, himself embarked on Easter-day, and prosperously reached the continent. Not long after, he had very nearly experienced the malignity of adverse fortune; for the king endeavoured to intercept him by treachery, at the instigation of one William de Ipres. The earl, however, informed of it by one of the accomplices, avoided the snare prepared for him, and absented himself from the palace, whither he was repeatedly invited, for several days. The king, troubled at having succeeded so little by his artifices, and thinking to effect his design by cunning, endeavoured, by a serene countenance and gratuitous confession, to extenuate the enormity of his crime. He swore, in words framed at the earl's pleasure, never again to give countenance to such an outrage; and still more to recover his good graces, he confirmed his oath, by Hugh, archbishop of Rouen, giving his hand to Robert. This he did, it is true; but he never bestowed his unreserved friendship on that man, of whose power he was ever apprehensive. Thus, in his presence, he would pleasantly and affably call him "earl;" when he was absent, he would vilify him, and would deprive him of such portions of his estates as he was able. Robert, too, artfully eluding his duplicity, disguised his feelings, and allowing the king to depart peaceably to his kingdom, continued in Normandy, intent on his own concerns. Wherefore while Stephen, perplexed by many commotions in England, and first attacking one, and then another, justly verified what was said of Ishmael, that the hands of all were against him, and his hand against all, Robert passed that whole year in Normandy in perfect quiet. The king pointedly, as it is reported, used frequently to say of his rebellious subjects, "Since they have elected me king, why do they desert me? By the birth of God, I will never be called a fallen king!" Robert, placed as it were on an eminence, watched the event of circumstances, and earnestly revolved how he might escape, before God and man, the imputation of falsifying the oath he had sworn to his sister.

§ 18. [A.D. 1138.] In the year of our Lord one thousand one hundred and thirty-eight, England was shaken with intestine commotions. For many persons, emboldened to illegal acts, either by nobility of descent or by ambition, or rather by the unbridled heat of youth, were not ashamed, some to demand castles, others estates, and indeed whatever came into their fancy, from the king: and when he delayed complying with their requests, alleging the dismemberment of his kingdom, or that others would make similar claims, or were already in possession of them; they, becoming enraged immediately, fortified their castles against him, and drove away large booties from his lands. Nor, indeed, was his spirit at all broken by the revolt of any, but attacking them suddenly in different places, he always concluded matters more to his own disadvantage than to theirs; for, after many great but fruitless labours, he gained from them, by the grant of honours or castles, a feigned and temporary peace. He created likewise many earls,[1] where there had been none before, appropriating to them possessions and rents, which rightfully belonged to the crown. They were the more greedy in asking, and he the more profuse in giving, because a rumour was pervading England, that Robert earl of Gloucester, who was in Normandy, would shortly espouse the cause of his sister, after first renouncing his fealty to the king. This report was in fact well founded: for shortly after Pentecost, despatching some of his people to Stephen, from Normandy, he, according to ancient usage, renounced his fealty and friendship, and annulled his homage; assigning as a just reason for so doing, that the king had illegally aspired to the kingdom, and neglected his plighted faith to him, not to say absolutely belied it: and, moreover, that he himself had acted contrary to law; who, after the oath sworn to his sister, had not blushed to do homage to another during her lifetime. Doubtless also his mind was biassed by the answers of many ecclesiastics, whom he had consulted upon the subject; who declared that he could by no means pass the present life without ignominy, nor deserve the happiness of the next, if he violated the oath made to paternal affection. In addition to this, he contemplated the tenor of the papal decree, commanding obedience to the oath taken in the presence of his father; a copy of which decree I shall be careful to give in my next book. Robert, who had imbibed knowledge by a copious draught from the fount of science, was aware that these things would be of great advantage to him hereafter. But the king, indignant at the spirit of the earl, deprived him, as far as he was able, of all his possessions in England, and levelled some of his castles to the ground. Bristol alone remained, which not only expelled the enemy, but even harassed the king by frequent incursions. But as it may suffice to have brought the first book of the history of our own times from the return of the empress to her father (after the death of her husband), down to this period, I shall now begin the second, from the year in which this heroine came to England, to assert her right against Stephen.

[1] Earls, till this time, had apparently been official; each having charge of a county, and receiving certain emoluments therefrom: but these created by Stephen seem to have been often merely titulary, with endowments out of the demesnes of the crown. Rob. Montensis calls these persons Pseudo-Comites, imaginary earls, and observes that Stephen had completely impoverished the crown by his liberalities to them. Henry the Second, however, on being firmly seated on the throne, recalled their grants of crown lands, and expelled them from the kingdom.

THE SECOND BOOK OF WILLIAM OF MALMESBURY'S
HISTORY OF HIS OWN TIMES.

BOOK II.

§ 91. [A.D. 1139.] In the year of our Lord's incarnation, one thousand one hundred and thirty-nine, the venom of malice, which had long been nurtured in the breast of Stephen, at length openly burst forth. Rumours were prevalent in England, that earl Robert was on the very eve of coming from Normandy with his sister; and when, under such an expectation, many persons revolted from the king, not only in inclination but in deed, he avenged himself for this 'injury at the cost of numbers. He also, to his disgrace as a king, seized many when at court, through mere suspicion of hostility to him, and obliged them to surrender their castles, and accede to any conditions he prescribed. There were at that time two very powerful bishops in England, Roger of Salisbury, and his fraternal nephew, Alexander of Lincoln. Alexander had built the castle of Newark, as he said, for the defence and dignity of the bishopric. Roger, who wished to manifest his magnificence by building, had erected extensive castles at Shireburn, and more especially at Devizes. At Malmesbury, even in the churchyard, and scarcely a stone's throw from the principal church, he had begun a castle. He had gotten into his custody the castle of Salisbury, which, being royal property, he had obtained from king Henry, and surrounded with a wall. Some powerful laymen, hurt at the probability of being surpassed by the clergy in extent of riches and magnitude of their towns, took offence at this, and fostered the latent wound of envy in their bosoms. Wherefore they poured forth their imagined grievances to the king; observing that the bishops, regardless of their order, were mad for erecting castles : that none could doubt but that they were designed for the overthrow of the king; for as soon as the empress should arrive, they would, induced doubtless by the recollection of her father's kindness to them, immediately greet their sovereign with the surrender of their fortresses : that therefore they ought to be prevented, and compelled to give up their strongholds ; otherwise the king would repent too late, when he saw in the power of the enemy that which, had he been wise, he might have applied to his own purpose. Such were the frequent insinuations of the nobility. The king, though far too partial to them, for some time pretended not to listen to what gratified his ear so much ; assuaging the bitterness of delay, either by his respect for the piety of the bishops, or, as I rather think, from apprehension of the odium he might incur by seizing their castles. Finally, he only postponed the execution of what the nobles had urged him to, till an opportunity presented itself for his purpose ; which was as follows :

§ 20. A great assembly of the nobles being held at Oxford about the eighth of the kalends of July [June 24], the prelates above-mentioned also repaired thither. The bishop of Salisbury set out on this expedition with great reluctance ; for I heard him speaking to the following purport : " By my Lady St. Mary, I know not why, but my heart revolts at this journey ; this I am sure of, that I shall be of much the same service at court as a foal is in battle :" thus did his mind forbode future evils. Here, as though fortune would seem subservient to the king's wishes, a quarrel arose between the servants of the bishops and those of Alan, earl of Brittany, about a right to quarters, which had a melancholy termination ; as the bishop of Salisbury's retainers, then sitting at table, left their meal unfinished and rushed to the contest. At first, they contended with reproaches, afterwards with swords. The domestics of Alan were put to flight, and his nephew nearly killed : nor was the victory gained without bloodshed on the bishops' side ; for many were wounded, and one knight[1] even slain. The king, eagerly seizing the opportunity, ordered the bishops to be convened by his old instigators, that they might make satisfaction to his court, as their people had infringed his peace : and that this satisfaction should be, the delivery of the keys of their castles, as pledges of their fidelity. Though prepared to make compensation, they hesitated at the surrender of their fortresses ; and in consequence, lest they should depart, he ordered them into close confinement. So he took bishop Roger unfettered, but the chancellor, the nephew, (or as it was reported, more than the nephew,) of the bishop, in chains, to Devizes ; intending, if he could, to get possession of the castle, which was erected at great and almost incalculable expense, not, as the prelate himself used to say, for the ornament, but as the real fact is, to the detriment of the church. At the first summons, the castles of Salisbury, Shireburn, and Malmesbury, were yielded to the king ; Devizes also surrendered at the end of three days, after the bishop had voluntarily enjoined himself abstinence from all food, that by his personal sufferings he might work upon the mind of the bishop of Ely, who had taken possession of it.[2] Nor did Alexander bishop of Lincoln act more perseveringly ; for he purchased his liberty by the surrender of his castles of Newark and Sleaford.[3]

§ 21. This transaction on the part of the king gave rise to the expression of many different opinions. Some observed that the bishops were justly dispossessed of their castles, as they had built them in opposition to the injunction of the canons ; they ought to be preachers of peace, not builders of houses which might be a refuge for evil-doers. Such was the doctrine enforced, with ampler reasons

---

[1] The term "miles" is very ambiguous : sometimes it is a knight ; sometimes a trooper ; sometimes a soldier generally. In later times it signified almost always a knight ; but in Malmesbury it seems mostly a horseman, probably of the higher order.

[2] The author of the " Gesta Stephani " says, the king ordered both bishops to be kept without food, and threatened, moreover, to hang the son of bishop Roger. Gest. Stephani, 944. The continuator of Flor. Wigorn. adds, that one was confined in the crib of an ox-lodge, the other in a vile hovel, A.D. 1138.

[3] Castellorum, Newarke, et Esleford, MS. E.

and discourses, by Hugh archbishop of Rouen; as far as his eloquence extended, the strenuous champion of the king.   Others took
the opposite side of the question; among whom was Henry bishop
of Winchester, legate of England from the papal see, and brother to
king Stephen, as I have said before, whom neither fraternal affection nor fear of danger could turn aside from the path of truth.   He
spake to this effect: " If the bishops had in anything overpassed
the bounds of justice, the judging them did not pertain to the king,
but to the ecclesiastical canons; that they ought not to be deprived
of any possession but by a public and ecclesiastical council; that
the king had not acted from zealous regard to right, but with a view
to his own advantage; as he had not restored the castles to the
churches, at whose expense, and on whose land, they were built, but
had delivered them to laymen, and those by no means of religious
character."   Though the legate made these declarations, not only
privately, but publicly also before the king, and urged him to the
liberation and restitution of the bishops, yet being entirely dis-
regarded, he lost his labour.   In consequence, deeming it proper to
resort to canonical power, he summoned his brother, without delay,
to be present at a council he intended to hold at Winchester, on
the fourth of the kalends of September [Aug. 29].

§ 22. On the appointed day, almost all the bishops of England,
with Theobald archbishop of Canterbury, who had succeeded
William, came to Winchester.   Turstin, archbishop of York, excused himself, on account of the malady with which he was afflicted;
for he was so enfeebled as to be hardly able to guide his steps: the
others apologized for their absence, by letter, by reason of the war.
The bull of pope Innocent was first read in the council, whereby, even
from the kalends of March, if I rightly remember, he had enjoined the
administration of his anxious charge to the lord bishop of Winchester, as legate in England.   This was received with much good-
will, as the bishop had shown his forbearance, by the lapse of time,
and had not proclaimed himself legate with precipitate vanity.   Next
followed, in the council, his address, in the Latin tongue, directed
to the learned, on the disgraceful detention of the bishops; of whom
the bishop of Salisbury had been seized in a chamber of the palace,
Lincoln in his lodgings, and Ely, fearing a similar treatment, had
escaped the calamity by a hasty retreat to Devizes: he observed, that it was a dreadful crime, that the king should be so
led away by sinister persons, as to have ordered violent hands to be
laid on his subjects, more especially bishops, in the security of his
court; that, to the king's disgrace, was to be added the offence
against God, in despoiling the churches of their possessions, under
pretext of the criminality of the prelates; that the king's outrage against the law of God was matter of such pain to him, that
he had rather himself suffer grievous injury, both in person and
property, than have the episcopal dignity so basely humiliated;
moreover, that the king, being repeatedly admonished to amend his
fault, had at last not refused that the council should be summoned:
that, therefore, the archbishop and the rest should deliberate what
was proper to be done; and he would not be wanting to execute

the sentence of the council, either through regard to the friendship of the king, who was his brother, or loss of property, or even danger of life.

§ 23. When he had gradually expatiated on these matters, the king, not distrusting his cause, sent certain earls[1] into the council, to demand wherefore he was summoned. The legate briefly replied : That, when he recollected he was in subjection to the faith of Christ, he ought not to be displeased, if, when guilty of a crime such as the present age had never witnessed, he was required, by the ministers of Christ, to make satisfaction ; that it was the act of heathen nations to imprison bishops, and divest them of their possessions ; that they should tell his brother, therefore, that if he would deign a patient assent to his advice, he would give him such, by the authority of God, as neither the church of Rome, nor the French king's court, nor even earl Theobald, their common brother, a man of surpassing sense and piety, could reasonably oppose; but such as they ought favourably to embrace; that, at present, the king would act advisedly, if he would either account for his conduct, or submit to canonical judgment ; it was, moreover, a debt he owed, to favour the church, by whose fostering care, not by military force, he had been promoted to the kingdom.   The earls retiring after this speech, returned shortly with an answer prepared.   They were accompanied by one Alberic de Ver, a man deeply versed in legal affairs.   He reported the king's answer, and aggravated as much as possible the case of bishop Roger, for bishop Alexander, whom he supported, had departed ; but this he did with moderation and without using opprobrious language, though some of the earls, standing by, repeatedly interrupted his harangue, by casting reproaches on the bishop.

§ 24. The sum of what Alberic had to allege, was as follows : That bishop Roger had greatly injured king Stephen ; that he seldom came to court but his people, presuming on his power, excited tumults ; that they had frequently at other places, and very lately at Oxford, attacked the attendants, and even the nephew of earl Alan, as well as the servants of Hervy de Liuns, a man of such high nobility, and so extremely haughty, that he had never deigned to visit England, though king Henry had invited him ; that the injury, therefore, of such violence having been offered him, doubly recoiled on king Stephen, through respect to whom he had come hither ; that the bishop of Lincoln had been the author of the tumult excited by his followers, from ancient enmity to Alan ; that the bishop of Salisbury secretly favoured the king's enemies, though he disguised his subtlety for the moment ; that the king had discovered this beyond all doubt, from many circumstances ; more especially, however, from the said bishop having refused permission to Roger de Mortimer, with the king's soldiers whom he was conducting, when under the greatest apprehensions from the garrison of Bristol, to continue even a single night at Malmesbury ; that it was in every

---

[1] It has before been related that Stephen made many earls, where there had been none before; these seem the persons intended by Malmesbury in many places, when speaking of some of the king's adherents.

person's mouth, that as soon as the empress should arrive, he would
join her party, with his nephews and his castles ; that Roger, in
consequence, was made captive, not as a bishop, but as the king's
servant, who had administered his affairs and received his wages ;
that the king had not taken their castles by violence, but that both
bishops had surrendered them voluntarily, to escape the punishment
due to the disturbance they had excited in the court ; that the king
had found some trifling sums of money in the castles, which must
lawfully belong to himself, as bishop Roger had collected it from the
revenues of the exchequer, in the times of his uncle and predecessor,
king Henry ; that the bishop had readily relinquished this money,
as well as the castles, through consciousness of his offences, of which
the king did not want witnesses ; that, therefore, it was his will
that the conditions entered into by himself and the bishops should
remain in force.

§ 25. It was rejoined, by bishop Roger, in opposition to the
speech of Alberic, that he had never been the minister of king
Stephen, nor had he received his wages.   This spirited man, too,
who blushed at being cast down by adversity, threatened, that if he
could not have justice from that council, for the property which
had been wrested from him, he would seek it in the audience of an
higher court.   The legate, mildly, as usual, observed, that every
allegation against the bishops ought to be made, and the truth of it
inquired into, in an ecclesiastical court, before passing sentence,
contrary to the canons, on innocent persons ; that the king ought,
therefore, to do as was incumbent in civil courts, that is, re-invest
the bishops with their own property, otherwise, being disseized, by
the law of nations they would not plead.

§ 26. Many arguments of this kind being used on both sides,
the cause, at the king's request, was adjourned to the next day ;
then, on the morrow, prolonged still a day farther, till the arrival of
the archbishop of Rouen.   When he came, while all were anxious
to hear what he had to allege, he said he was willing to allow the
bishops their castles, if they could prove by the canons that they
ought justly to possess them ; but as they were not able to do this,
it was the height of impudence to contend against the canons.
" And admitting," said he, " that it be just for them to possess
castles, yet most assuredly, as the times are eventful, all chiefs,
after the custom of other nations, ought to deliver up the keys of
their fortifications to the will of the king, who is bound to wage war
for the common security."   Thus the whole plea of the bishops
was shaken : for, either according to the decrees of the canons, it
was unjust for them to have castles ; or, if that were allowed by the
king's indulgence, they ought to yield to the emergency of the times,
and give up the keys.

§ 27. To this the aforesaid pleader, Alberic, added, that, it had
been signified to the king, that the bishops murmured among themselves, and had even made preparation for some of their party to
proceed to Rome against him.   " And this," said he, " the king
advises that none of you presume to do ; for if any person shall go
from England to any place, in opposition to him and to the dignity

of his kingdom, perhaps his return may not be so easy. Moreover, he, as he sees himself aggrieved, of his own accord summons you to Rome."

§ 28. When the king had sent such a message, partly advising, and partly threatening, it was perceived what was his design. In consequence, the council broke up, as he would not submit to canonical censure, and the bishops deemed it unadvisable to enforce it against him for two reasons: first, because it was a rash act to excommunicate the king without the knowledge of the pope; secondly, because they understood, or some of them even saw, that swords were unsheathed around them. It was no longer a joking matter, but a struggle for life and death. The legate and the archbishop, still, however, were anxiously observant of their duty. They humbly prostrated themselves before the king in his chamber, entreating him to take pity on the church, and to consider his soul and his reputation; and that he would not suffer a schism to be made between the empire and the priesthood. Although he, in some measure, removed the odium of his former conduct, by condescendingly rising to them, yet, prevented by ill advice, he carried none of his fair promises into effect.

§ 29. The council broke up on the kalends of September [Sept. 1]; and on the day previous to the kalends of October [Sept. 30], earl Robert, having at length surmounted every cause of delay, arrived with the empress, his sister, in England, relying on the protection of God and the observance of his lawful oath; but with a much smaller military force than any other person would have required for so perilous an enterprise; for he had not with him, at that time, more than one hundred and forty horsemen. My assertion is supported by persons of veracity; and did it not look like flattery, I would say that he was not inferior to Julius Cæsar, at least in resolution, whom Livy[1] relates to have had but five cohorts, when he began the civil war, and with which he attacked the world. But the comparison between Julius and Robert is invidious; for Julius, an alien to the true faith, reposed his hope on his good fortune, as he used to say, and the valour of his legions; Robert, celebrated for Christian piety, relied only on the assistance of the Holy Spirit, and the Lady St. Mary. The former had partisans in Gaul, in parts of Germany, and Brittany; and had attached to him, by means of presents, all the Roman people, with the exception of the senate; the latter, with the exception of a very few who regarded their plighted oath, found the nobility in England either opposing or affording him no assistance. He landed, then, at Arundel, and, for a time, delivered his sister into the safe keeping, as he supposed, of her mother-in-law, whom Henry, as I have before related, had married on the death of the empress's mother. He himself proceeded through the hostile country to Bristol, accompanied, as I have heard, by scarcely twelve horsemen, and was joined in the midst of his journey by Brian the earl's son from Wallingford. Nor was it long ere he learnt that his sister had quitted Arundel; for her mother-in-law, through female

[1] It would seem from this passage, that he had seen Livy's work entire.

inconstancy, had broken the faith she had repeatedly pledged by
messengers sent into Normandy. The king, therefore, placed the
empress under the care of Henry bishop of Winchester, and
Waleran earl of Meulan for safe-conduct; a favour never denied
to the most inveterate enemy by honourable soldiers. Waleran,
indeed, declined going farther than Calne; but the bishop continued his route. The earl, therefore, quickly collecting his troops,
came to the boundary appointed by the king, and placed his sister
in safer quarters at Bristol. She was afterwards received into
Gloucester by Milo, who held the castle of that city under the earl
in the time of king Henry, doing him homage and swearing fidelity
to him; for this is the chief city of his county.

§ 30. On the nones of October [Oct. 7] one Robert Fitz-Hubert,
a savage barbarian, by night clandestinely entering the castle of
Malmesbury, which bishop Roger had inauspiciously founded, and
burning the town, boasted of the deed, as though he had gained
a great triumph. But, within a fortnight, his joy was at an end,
being put to flight by the king. Stephen, in the meantime, commanded possession to be kept of the castle, until, on the restoration
of peace, it might be destroyed. The king, moreover, before he
came to Malmesbury, had occupied and placed a garrison in a small
fortress called Cerney, belonging to the aforesaid Milo. In consequence, thinking that he should be equally successful elsewhere as
at that place and at Malmesbury, he assailed a castle called Trow-
bridge, belonging to Humphrey de Bohun, who was on the side of
the empress, but he departed without success.

§ 31. The whole country, then, around Gloucester, to the extremity of Wales, partly by force, and partly by favour, in the
course of the remaining months of that year, gradually espoused
the side of the empress. The owners of certain castles, securing
themselves within their fastnesses, waited the issue of events. The
city of Hereford was taken without difficulty; the few soldiers,
who, determining on resistance, had thrown themselves into the
castle, being blockaded therein. The king drew nigh, if possible,
to devise means for their assistance; but, frustrated in his attempt,
he retired with disgrace. He also approached Bristol, and going
beyond it, burnt the neighbourhood around Dunstore, leaving
nothing, as far as he was able, which could afford sustenance for
his enemies, or advantage to any one.

§ 32. On the third of the ides of December [Dec. 11], death
kindly relieved Roger bishop of Salisbury from the quartan ague
which had long afflicted him. They assert that his sickness was
brought upon him through grief at the severe and repeated injuries
he had received from king Stephen. To me it appears that God exhibited him to the wealthy as an example of the mutability of fortune,
in order that they should not trust in uncertain riches, which, as
the apostle[1] says, "while some have coveted, they have made ship-
wreck of their faith." He first ingratiated himself with prince
Henry, who became afterwards king, by his prudence in the
management of domestic matters, and by restraining the excesses

[1] 1 Tim. i. 19.

of his household. For, before his accession, Henry had been careful
and economical in his expenses, compelled thereto by the scantiness
of his resources, and the illiberal treatment of his brothers, William
and Robert. Knowing his disposition in this way, Roger had deserved so well of him in his time of need, that, when he came to the
throne, he denied him scarcely anything he thought proper to ask; he
gave him estates, churches, prebends, entire abbeys of monks; and,
lastly, committed even the kingdom to his fidelity : he made him
chancellor in the beginning of his reign, and not long after, bishop
of Salisbury. Roger, therefore, decided causes ; he regulated the
expenditure ; he had charge of the treasury. Such were his occupations when the king was in England ; such, without associate or
inspector, when he resided in Normandy, which took place repeatedly, and for a long time together. And not only the king, but
the nobility, even those who were secretly stung with envy at his
good fortune, and more especially the ministers and debtors of the
king, gave him almost whatever he could fancy. If there was anything contiguous to his property which might be advantageous to
him, he would directly extort it, either by entreaty or purchase ; or,
if that failed, by force. With unrivalled magnificence in their con-
struction, as our times may recollect, he erected splendid mansions
on all his estates ; in merely maintaining which, the labour of his
successors shall toil in vain. His cathedral he dignified to the
utmost with matchless ornaments, and buildings on which no
expense was spared. It was truly wonderful to behold in this man
what abundant power attended him in every kind of dignity, and
flowed, as it were, to his hand. How great was the glory, (indeed,
what could exceed it?) that he should have made his two nephews—
by virtue of the education which he bestowed upon them, men of
noted learning and industry—bishops ; and not of mean sees, but
of Lincoln and Ely, than which I know not whether there be more
opulent in England ! He was sensible of his power, and, somewhat
more harshly than became such a character, abused the favours of
Heaven. Lastly, as the poet observes of some rich man,[1]

"He builds, destroys, and changes square for round,"

so Roger attempted to turn abbeys into bishoprics, and bishoprics
into abbeys. The most ancient monasteries of Malmesbury and
Abbotsbury, he annexed, as far as he was able, to his see ; he
changed the priory of Shireburn, which is subject to the bishop of
Salisbury, into an abbey; and the abbey of Hortun was forthwith
dissolved and united to it. These events took place in the time of
king Henry, under whom, as I have observed, his prosperity reached
its zenith ; for under Stephen, as I have before related, it began to
decline; except that in the beginning of his reign, he obtained for
one of his nephews the chancellorship; for the other the office of
treasurer ; and for himself the town of Malmesbury ; the king re-
peating often to his companions, " By the birth of God, I would
give him half England, if he asked for it ; till the time be ripe, he
shall tire of asking, ere I tire of giving." But fortune, who, in

[1] Horat. Epist. I. i. 100.

former times, had flattered him so long and so transcendently, at
last cruelly pierced him with her scorpion-sting.   Such was that
instance, when he saw those whom he dearly regarded, wounded,
and his most favoured knight killed before his face ; the next day,
himself, as I said before, and his nephews, very powerful bishops,
the first compelled to fly, the second detained, and the third,
a young man to whom he was greatly attached, bound with chains;
on the surrender of his castles, his treasures pillaged, and himself
afterwards, in the council, loaded with the most disgraceful reproaches : finally, when he was on his death-bed at Salisbury, the
residue of his money and utensils, which he had placed upon the
altar for the purpose of completing the church, were carried off
against his will.   The height of his calamity was, I think, a circumstance which even I cannot help commiserating ; that, though
he appeared wretched to many, yet there were very few who pitied
him ; so much envy and hatred had his excessive power drawn on
him, and undeservedly, too, from some of those very persons whom
he had advanced to honour.

§ 33.   In the year of the Incarnate Word one thousand one
hundred and forty, the monks of those abbeys, which Roger had
unjustifiably usurped, waiting on the king, were permitted to enjoy
their ancient privileges, and abbots, as formerly.   John, a monk of
that place, a man highly celebrated for the affability of his manners
and the liberality of his mind, was elected abbot of Malmesbury by
the monks, according to the tenor of the privilege which St. Ald-
helm had obtained from pope Sergius four hundred and sixty-six
years before, and had caused to be confirmed by the kings, Ina of
the West Saxons, and Ethelred of the Mercians.   The legate
approved the claim, but disapproved of the person ; for he could
not be induced to believe that the king had consented to the election but by a gift in money.   And, indeed, a small sum had been
promised, on the score of liberating the church, not for the election
of the person.   Wherefore, John, though removed by a premature
death within the year, still left a lasting and laudable memory of
himself to all succeeding ages.   For no monk of that place, I confess the truth, would have pursued a task of such difficulty, had not
John begun it.   Wherefore let his successors be praised, if they
shall preserve the liberty of that church ; he certainly rescued it
from thraldom.

§ 34.   The whole of this year was embittered by the horrors of
war.   There were many castles throughout England, each defending,
or more properly speaking, laying waste, its neighbourhood.   The
garrisons drove off from the fields, both sheep and cattle, sparing
neither churches nor churchyards.   Seizing[1] such of the vavas-
sours[2] and country-people as were reputed to be possessed of
money, they compelled them, by extreme torture, to promise
whatever they thought fit.   Plundering the houses of the wretched
husbandmen, even to their very beds, they cast them into prison ;

---

[1] MS. E. adds from "seizing" to "thought fit."
[2] The meaning of "vavassour" is very various; here it seems to imply what
we call a yeoman.

nor did they liberate them, but on their giving everything they possessed, or could by any means scrape together, for their release. Many calmly expired in the midst of torments inflicted to compel them to ransom themselves, bewailing, which was all they could do, their miseries to God. At the instance of the earl, indeed, the legate, with the bishops, repeatedly excommunicated all violators of churchyards and plunderers of churches, and those who laid violent hands on men in holy or monastic orders, or their servants; but this his attention profited but little. It was distressing, therefore, to see England, once the fondest cherisher of peace and the signal home of tranquillity, reduced to such a pitch of misery, that not even the bishops or monks could pass in safety from one town to another. Under king Henry, many foreigners, who had been driven from home by the commotions of their native land, were accustomed to resort to England, and rest in quiet under his fostering protection; in Stephen's time, numbers of freebooters from Flanders and Brittany flocked to England, in expectation of rich pillage. Meanwhile, the earl of Gloucester conducted himself with caution, and his most earnest endeavours were directed to gaining conquests with the smallest loss to his adherents. Such of the English nobility as he could not prevail upon to regard the obligation of their oath, he held it sufficient if he could so restrain, that, if they did not assist, they would not injure the cause; being willing, according to the saying of the comic writer, to do what he could, when he could not do what he would. But when he saw the opportunity present itself, he strenuously performed the duty both of soldier and of general; more especially he valiantly subdued those strongholds, which were of signal detriment to the cause he had espoused; that[1] is to say, Harpetrey, which king Stephen had taken from certain soldiers of the earl before he came to England, and many others; Sudley, Cerney, which the king had garrisoned, as I have said; and the castle which Stephen had fortified over against Wallingford he levelled to the ground. He also, in these difficult times, created his brother Rainald, earl of Cornwall. Nor, indeed, did the king show less spirit in performing the duties of his station; for he omitted no occasion of repeatedly beating off his adversaries, and defending his own possessions. But he failed of success, and his affairs grew worse for lack of justice. Dearth of provisions, too, increased by degrees; and the scarcity of good money was so great, from being counterfeited, that sometimes, out of ten or more shillings, hardly a dozen pence would be received. The king himself was reported to have ordered the weight of the penny, as established in king Henry's time, to be reduced, because, having exhausted the vast treasures of his predecessor, he was unable to provide for the expense of so many soldiers. All things, then, became venal in England; and churches and abbeys were no longer secretly, but even publicly, exposed to sale.

§ 35. During this year, in Lent, on the thirteenth of the kalends of April [March 20], at the ninth hour of the fourth day of the week,

[1] MS. E. inserts from "that" to "the ground."

there was an eclipse, throughout England, as I have heard. With us, indeed, and with all our neighbours, the obscuration of the sun was so remarkable, that persons sitting at table, as it then happened almost everywhere, (for it was Lent,[1]) at first feared that chaos was come again; afterwards learning its cause, they went out, and beheld the stars around the sun. It was thought and said by many, not untruly, that the king would not continue a year in the government.

§ 36. In the following week, that is, during the time of the Passion, on the seventh of the kalends of April [March 26], the fore-mentioned barbarian,[2] Robert Fitz-Hubert, a character well calculated for the stratagems of war, surprised the castle of Devizes.[3] He was a man by far the most cruel of any within the circle of this age's memory; and blasphemous, also, towards God: he used voluntarily to boast of having been present at a place where twenty-four monks were burnt, together with the church; declaring, that he, too, would frequently do the like in England, and grieve God, by the plunder of the church of Wilton, and the destruction of Malmesbury, with the slaughter of all its monks; that he would return them this good office, because they had admitted the king, to his disadvantage; for of this he accused them, though without foundation. I myself have heard, when, at any time, which was extremely rare indeed, he liberated his captives without torture, and they thanked him for it, on the part of God, I have heard him, I say, reply; " Never let God owe me any thanks." He used to expose his prisoners, naked and rubbed with honey, to the burning heat of the sun; thereby exciting flies, and other insects of that kind, to sting them. But, having now got possession of Devizes, he hesitated not to boast, that he should gain, by means of this castle, the whole district from Winchester to London; and that he would send to Flanders for soldiers to defend him. While meditating, however, such a scheme, Divine vengeance overtook him, through the agency of John Fitz-Gilbert, a man of surprising subtlety, who held the castle at Marlborough: for being thrown into chains by him, because he refused to surrender Devizes to his sovereign, the empress, he was hanged, like a common thief. Wonderful was the judgment of God on this sacrilegious wretch, that he should meet with such an ignominious end, not from the king, to whom he was inimical, but from the very persons he appeared to favour. The authors of his death ought worthily to be extolled, for having freed the country from such a pest, and justly dispatched an intestine enemy.

§ 37. In the same year, during Pentecost [May 26], the king resided at London, in the Tower, attended only by the bishop of Sees, for the others disdained, or feared, to come thither. Some little time after, by the mediation of the legate, a conference was appointed between the empress and the king, that, if possible, by God's help, peace might be restored. The conference was held near

---

[1] The passage within brackets occurs only in E.   [2] See § 30, p. 400.
[3] This he effected by means of scaling ladders, made of thongs of leather. Gest. Stephani, 951.

Bath; on the part of the empress were sent her brother Robert, and others of her friends; on the king's, the legate, the archbishop, and also the queen.   But they wasted words and time, to no purpose, and departed without being able to conclude a peace.   Nor was the ground of separation equal on both sides, as the empress, more inclined to justice, had declared, that she was not averse to the decision of the church; but the king's party were averse to this, so long as they could make their ascendency over him answer their own purposes.   In September following, the legate, who knew that it was the especial duty of his office to restore peace, undertaking the toil of a foreign voyage for its accomplishment, hastened to sail over to France.   After a long and anxious discussion, for tranquillizing England, had taken place, between the king of France, count Thibaut, and many of the clergy, he returned, nearly at the end of November, bringing back counsels wholesome for the country, could they have been carried into effect.   And indeed the empress and the earl assented to them immediately, but the king delayed from day to day, and finally rejected them altogether.   Upon this, at last, the legate discontinued his exertions, waiting, like the rest, for the issue of events: for what avails it to swim against the stream? and, as some one observes, " To seek odium only by one's labours is the height of madness."

PREFACE TO BOOK III.

I NOW attempt[1] to give a clue to the mazy labyrinth of events and transactions which occurred in England, during the year one thousand one hundred and forty-one,[2] lest posterity, through my neglect, should be unacquainted with them; as it is of service, to know the volubility of fortune, and the mutability of human estate, God only permitting or ordaining them.   And, as the moderns greatly and deservedly blame our predecessors, for having left no memorial of themselves or their transactions, since the days of Beda, I think I ought to be very favourably regarded by my readers, if they judge rightly, for determining to remove this reproach from our times.

THE THIRD BOOK OF WILLIAM OF MALMESBURY'S HISTORY OF HIS OWN TIMES.

BOOK III.

§ 38.   KING STEPHEN had peaceably departed from the county of Lincoln before Christmas, and had augmented the honours of the earl of Chester, and of his brother; of whom the earl, long since, in the time of king Henry, had been married to the daughter of the

---

[1] Here the MSS. fluctuate as to the commencement of the third book, of which, in some, this is called the prologue.

[2] Several MSS. (D. E 2. L 2.), as well as Saville's printed copy, read 1142, but one (E J.) has 1141, which is right.

earl of Gloucester. In the meanwhile, the citizens of Lincoln, who
wished to acquire great favour with the king, certified him by a
message, when resident in London, that the two brothers had taken
up their abode in security, in the castle of that city; and that, sus-
pecting nothing less than the arrival of the king, they might be very
easily surprised, while they themselves would provide that he should
get possession of the castle as secretly as possible. As Stephen
never wished to neglect any opportunity of augmenting his power,
he gladly repaired thither. In consequence, the brothers were surprised, and besieged, even in the Christmas holidays. This step
appeared unjustifiable to many, because, as I have observed, he had
left them before the festival, without any suspicion of enmity; nor had
he, even now, after ancient usage, abjured his friendship with them,
which they call " defying." However, the earl of Chester, though
surrounded with imminent dangers, adroitly escaped from the
castle. By what management this was accomplished, I know not;
whether through consent of some of the besiegers, or whether
because valour, when taken by surprise, frequently tries a variety of
methods, and often discovers a remedy for its emergencies. Not
content with his own escape, he earnestly deliberated, how to devise
the safety of his brother and of his wife, whom he had left in the
fortress. The more prudent mode seemed to be, to request assistance from his father-in-law, although he had long since offended
him, on many accounts; but principally because he appeared
staunch to neither party. He sent messengers, therefore, promising
eternal fidelity to the empress, if, induced more by affectionate
regard than any desert of his, he would rescue those from danger,
who were already in the very jaws of captivity.

§ 39. Unable to endure this indignity, the earl of Gloucester
readily assented. Weary of delay, too, as the fairest country was
harassed with intestine rapine and slaughter for the sake of two
persons, he preferred bringing the matter to an issue at once, would
God permit. He hoped also for the Divine assistance on his
undertaking, as the king had molested his son-in-law, without any
fault on his part; was at that moment besieging his daughter; and
had castellated the church of the holy mother of God, in Lincoln.
How much ought these things to weigh in the mind of a prince?
Would it not be better to die, and fall with honour, than endure so
marked a disgrace? For the sake then of avenging God, and his
sister, and liberating his relations, he entered on this perilous
undertaking. The supporters of his party readily accompanied
him; the major part of whom being deprived of their inheritances,
were instigated to hostility by rage at their losses, and the consciousness of their valour. However, during the whole extended
march from Gloucester to Lincoln, he studiously concealed his
intention, leaving all the army, with the exception of a very few, in
suspense, by his mysterious conduct.

§ 40. At length, on the day of the Purification of the blessed
Mary [Feb. 2], they arrived at the river flowing between the two
armies, called the Trent, which, from its springs, together with floods
of rain, had risen so high, that it could not possibly be forded. Here,

at last, disclosing his intention to his son-in-law, who had joined
him with a strong force, and to those he had brought with him, he
added, that he had long since made up his mind, never to be
induced to fly, be the emergency what it might; if they could not
conquer, they must die, or be taken.   All encouraged him to hope
the best; and wonderful to hear, though on the eve of hazarding
a battle, he swam over the rapid river I have mentioned, with the
whole of his party.   So great was the earl's ardour to put an end to
calamity, that he preferred risking extremities, to prolonging the
sufferings of the country.   The king, too, with many earls, and an
active body of cavalry, abandoning the siege, courageously presented himself for battle.   The royalists began the prelude to the
fight, which they call the "joust,"[1] as they were skilled in that
exercise; but when they saw that the consular party, if they may
be so called, did not attack from a distance, with lances, but at
close-quarters, with swords, and broke the king's ranks with violent
and determined onset, the earls, to a man, [2](for six of them had
entered the conflict together with the king,) consulted their safety
by flight.   A few barons of laudable fidelity and valour, who would
not desert him, even in his necessity, were made captive.   The
king, though he by no means wanted spirit to defend himself,
being at last attacked on every side by the earl of Gloucester's
soldiers, fell to the ground by a blow from a stone; but who was
the author of this deed is uncertain.   Thus, when all around him
were either taken or dispersed, he was compelled to yield to circumstances and become a captive.   On which the truly noble earl of
Gloucester commanded the king to be preserved uninjured, not
suffering him to be molested, even with a reproach; and the person,
whom he had just before fiercely attacked when dignified with the
sovereignty, he now calmly protected when subdued; that, the
tumults of anger and of joy being quieted, he might show kindness
to his relation, and respect the dignity of the diadem in the captive.
The citizens of Lincoln were slaughtered on all sides by the just
indignation of the victors, and without commiseration on the part
of the conquered, as they had been the origin and fomenters of this
calamity.

§ 41. The king, according to the custom of such as are called
captives, was presented to the empress, at Gloucester, by her brother,
and afterwards conducted to Bristol.   Here at first he was kept
with every mark of honour, except the liberty of going at large: but
in succeeding time, through the presumption of certain persons,
who said openly and contumeliously, that it did not behove the earl
to treat the king otherwise than they chose; and also, because it
was reported, that, having either eluded or bribed his keepers, he
had been found, more than once, beyond the appointed limits, more
especially in the night time, he was confined with fetters.

§ 42. In the meanwhile, both the empress and the earl dealt by
messengers with the legate his brother, that he should forthwith

[1] The joust signifies a contest between two persons, on horseback, with lances;
each singling out his opponent.
[2] The passage here within brackets occurs only in E.

receive her into the church,[1] and to the kingdom, as the daughter
of king Henry, to whom all England and Normandy had sworn
allegiance. This year, the first Sunday in Lent happened on the
fourteenth of the kalends of March [Feb. 16]. By means of nego-
tiators on both sides, the business was so far forwarded, that they
agreed to meet in conference, on an open plain on this side of
Winchester. They assembled, therefore, on the third Sunday in
Lent [March 2], a day dark and rainy, as though the fates would
portend a woful change in this affair. The empress swore, and
pledged her faith to the bishop, that all matters of importance in
England, and especially the bestowing of bishoprics and abbeys,
should be under his control, if he, with the holy church, would
receive her as sovereign, and observe perpetual fidelity towards her.
Her brother, Robert, earl of Gloucester, swore as she did, and
pledged his faith for her, as did also Brian Fitz-Count, lord
Marcher[2] of Wallingford, and Milo of Gloucester, afterwards earl
of Hereford, with some others. Nor did the bishop hesitate to
receive the empress as sovereign of England, and, together with
certain of his party, to pledge his faith, that so long as she did not
infringe the covenant, he would observe his fidelity to her. On
the morrow, which was the fifth of the nones of March [March 3],
a splendid procession being formed, she was received in the cathedral
of Winchester ; the bishop-legate conducting her on the right side,
and Bernard bishop of St. David's on the left. There were present
also, Alexander bishop of Lincoln, Robert of Hereford, Nigel of
Ely, Robert of Bath : the abbots, Ingulf of Abingdon, Edward of
Reading, Peter of Malmesbury, Gilbert of Gloucester, Roger of
Tewkesbury, and some others. In a few days, Theobald, archbishop
of Canterbury, came to the empress at Winchester, by invitation
of the legate : but he deferred swearing fealty to her, deeming it
beneath his reputation and character to change sides, till he had
consulted the king. In consequence, he, and many other prelates,
with some few of the laity, were allowed to visit Stephen and
converse with him ; and, graciously obtaining leave to submit to
the exigency of the times, they embraced the sentiments of the
legate. The empress passed Easter, which happened on the third
of the kalends of April [March 30], at Oxford ; the rest returned
to their respective homes.

§ 43. On the second day after the octaves of Easter [April 7], a
council began, with great parade, at Winchester, consisting of Theobald archbishop of Canterbury, all the bishops of England, and many
abbots ; the legate presiding. Such as were absent, accounted for
it by messengers and letters. As I was present at the holding of
this council, I will not deny posterity a true account of its proceedings : I perfectly remember that, on the same day, after the letters
were read by which some excused their absence, the legate called
the bishops apart, and discoursed with them in secret of his

---

[1] That is, as appears after, to acknowledge her publicly as their sovereign.

[2] Marchio. This latterly signified marquis in the sense we now use it; but in
Malmesbury's time, and long after, it denoted a guardian of the borders : hence
the lords marchers on the confines of Scotland and Wales; though it does not
appear very clearly how this should apply to Wallingford.

design; then the abbots, and, lastly, the archdeacons were summoned. Of his intention nothing transpired publicly, though what was to be done engrossed the minds and conversation of all.

§ 44. On the third day of the week [April 8], the speech of the legate ran nearly to this effect: "That, by the condescension of the pope, he acted as his vicegerent in England: wherefore, by his authority, the clergy of England were assembled at this council, to deliberate on the peace of the country, which was exposed to imminent danger: that, in the time of king Henry, his uncle, England had been the peculiar abode of peace; so that, by the activity, and spirit, and care of that most excellent man, not only the natives, of whatever power or dignity, dared make no disturbance; but, by his example, each neighbouring king and prince, also, yielded to peace, and either persuaded, or compelled, his subjects to do the like; moreover, that this king, some years before his death, had caused the whole realm of England, as well as the duchy of Normandy, to be engaged, by the oaths of all the bishops and barons, to his daughter, late the empress, (who was his only surviving issue by his former consort,) if he should fail of male offspring by the wife he had espoused from Lorrain: and adverse fortune," said he, "was envious of my most excellent uncle, and suffered him to die in Normandy without male issue. Therefore, as it seemed long to wait for a sovereign who delayed coming to England, (for she resided in Normandy,) we provided for the peace of the country, and my brother was allowed to reign. And although I gave myself as surety between him and God, that he would honour and advance the holy church, and uphold good, but abrogate evil laws; yet it grieves me to remember, it shames me to say, how he conducted himself in the kingdom; how justice ceased to be exerted against the daring; how all peace was annihilated, almost within the year: the bishops made captive, and compelled to give up their possessions; the abbeys sold; the churches robbed of their treasures; the counsels of the abandoned regarded, while those of the virtuous were postponed, or totally despised. You know how often I addressed him, both by myself, and the bishops, more especially in the council held last year for that purpose, and that I gained by it nothing but odium. Every one who shall think rightly must be aware, that I ought to love my mortal brother, but that I should still more regard the cause of my immortal Father. Wherefore, since God has exercised his judgment on my brother, by permitting him, without my knowledge, to fall into the hands of the powerful, I have invited you all here to assemble by virtue of my legation, lest the kingdom should fall to decay through want of a sovereign. The case was yesterday agitated in private, before the major part of the English clergy, to whose right it principally pertains to elect the sovereign, and also to crown him. First, then, as is fitting, invoking God's assistance, we elect the daughter of that peaceful, that glorious, that rich, that good, that, in our times, incomparable king, as sovereign of England and Normandy, and promise her fidelity and support."

§ 45. When all present had either becomingly applauded his

sentiments, or by their silence assented thereto, he added : " We
have despatched messengers for the Londoners, (who, from the importance of their city in England, are nobles, as it were,) to meet
us on this business : and have sent them a safe-conduct : and I
trust they will not delay their arrival beyond to-morrow : wherefore
let us give them indulgence till that time."

§ 46. On the fourth day of the week [April 9], the Londoners
came ; and being introduced to the council, urged their cause, so
far as to say, that, they were sent from the fraternity, as they call it,
of London, not to contend, but to entreat that their lord the king
might be liberated from captivity ; that all the barons who had long
since been admitted to their fellowship, most earnestly solicited
this of the lord legate and the archbishop, as well as of all the
clergy who were present. The legate answered them copiously and
eloquently : and, that their request might be the less complied with,
the speech of the preceding day was repeated, with the addition, that
it did not become the Londoners, who were considered, as the chief
people of England, in the light of nobles, to side with those persons
who had deserted their lord in battle ; by whose advice, the king
had dishonoured the holy church ; and who, in fact, only appeared to favour the Londoners, that they might drain them of
their money.

§ 47. In the meantime, a certain person, whose name, if I
rightly remember, was Christian, a clerk belonging to the queen, as
I heard, rose up, and held forth a paper to the legate. He, having
silently perused it, exalted his voice to the highest pitch, and said,
that it was informal, and improper to be recited in so great an
assembly, especially of dignified and religious persons. For, among
other offensive and singular points, the signature of a person was
affixed to it, who, in the preceding year, at a similar council, had
attacked the venerable bishops with opprobrious language. The
legate thus baffling him, the clerk was not wanting to his mission,
but, with notable confidence, read the letter in their hearing ; of
which this was the purport :—" The queen earnestly entreated the
whole clergy assembled, and especially the bishop of Winchester,
the brother of her lord, to restore the said lord to his kingdom,
whom abandoned persons, and even such as were under homage to
him, had cast into chains." To this suggestion, the legate answered
to the same effect as to the Londoners. These conferring together,
declared, that they would relate the decree of the council to their
townsmen, and give it their support, as far as they were able. On
the fifth day of the week the council broke up, many of the royal
party having been first excommunicated ; more especially William
Martel, who had formerly been cup-bearer to king Henry, and was
at that time butler to Stephen ; for he had sorely exasperated the
legate, by intercepting and pilfering much of his property.

§ 48. It was now a work of great difficulty to soothe the minds
of the Londoners ; for, though these matters, as I have said, were
agitated immediately after Easter, yet was it only a few days before
the Nativity of St. John [June 24] that they would receive the
empress. At that time, great part of England readily submitted to

her government; her brother Robert was assiduously employed in promoting her dignity by every becoming method; kindly addressing the nobility, making many promises, and intimidating the adverse party, or even, by messengers, exhorting them to peace; and, already, restoring justice and the law of the land, and tranquillity, throughout every district which favoured the empress: and it is sufficiently notorious, that if his party had trusted to Robert's moderation and wisdom, it would not afterwards have experienced so melancholy a reverse. The lord legate, too, appeared of laudable fidelity, in furthering the interests of the empress. But, behold! at the very moment when she imagined she should get immediate possession of all England, everything was changed. The Londoners, ever suspicious and murmuring among themselves, now burst out into open expressions of hatred; and, as it is reported, even laid wait for their sovereign and her nobles. Aware of, and escaping, this plot, they gradually retired from the city, without tumult, and in a certain military order. The empress was accompanied by the legate, and David king of Scotland, the heroine's uncle, together with her brother Robert, who then, as at every other time, shared her fortune; and, in short, all her partisans, to a man, escaped in safety. The Londoners learning their departure, flew to their residence, and plundered everything which they had left in their haste.

§ 49. Not many days after, a misunderstanding arose between the legate and the empress, which may be justly considered as the melancholy cause of every subsequent evil in England. How this happened, I will explain. King Stephen had a son named Eustace, begotten on the daughter of Eustace earl of Boulogne. For king Henry, the father of the empress, (that I may go back somewhat, to acquaint posterity with the truth of these transactions,) had given Mary, the sister of his wife, the mother of this lady, in marriage to the aforesaid earl, as he was of noble descent, and equally renowned for prudence and for valour. By Mary, Eustace had no issue except a daughter, called Matilda. When she became marriageable, after the death of her father, the same truly magnificent king gave her in wedlock to his nephew Stephen, and also procured, by his care, the county of Boulogne for him, as he had before conferred on him that of Moritol in Normandy. The legate had justly proposed that these counties should be bestowed on his nephew Eustace, whom I mentioned, so long as his father should remain in captivity. This the empress altogether opposed, and it is doubtful whether she had not even promised them to others. Offended at the repulse, he kept from her court many days; and though repeatedly sent for, persisted in refusing to go thither. In the meanwhile, he held a friendly conference with the queen, his brother's wife, at Guildford, and being wrought upon by her tears and concessions, bent his mind to the liberation of Stephen: he also absolved, without consulting the bishops, all those of the king's party whom he had excommunicated in the council. His complaints against the empress were disseminated through England: that she wished to seize his person; that she observed nothing which she had sworn to him; that all the barons of England had performed their engagements towards her, but that she had violated hers, as she knew not how to use her prosperity with moderation.

§ 50. To allay, if possible, these commotions, the earl of Gloucester, with a small retinue, proceeded to Winchester; but failing in his endeavours, he returned to Oxford, where his sister had for some time established her residence. She, therefore, understanding, as well from what she was continually hearing, as from what she then learnt from her brother, that the legate had no friendly dispositions towards her, proceeded to Winchester with such forces as she could muster. Being immediately admitted into the royal castle, she sent messengers to the bishop, probably with good intentions, requesting that, as she was upon the spot, he would come to her without delay. He, not thinking it safe to go, deceived the messengers by an evasive answer; merely saying, " I will prepare myself:" and immediately he sent for all such as he knew were well-disposed to the king. In consequence, almost all the earls of England came; for they were full of youth and levity, and preferred military enterprise to peace. Besides, many of them were ashamed at having deserted the king in battle, as has been said before; and thought to wipe off the ignominy of having fled, by attending this meeting. Few, however, attended the empress: there were, David king of Scotland, Robert earl of Gloucester, Milo of Hereford, and some barons: for Ranulph earl of Chester came late, and to no purpose. To comprise, therefore, a long series of events within narrow limits: the roads on every side of Winchester were watched by the queen and the earls who had come with her, lest supplies should be brought in to those who had sworn fidelity to the empress. The town of Andover, also, was burnt. On the west, therefore, necessaries were procured but scantily, and with difficulty; some persons found on the road being intercepted, and either killed or maimed: while on the east, every avenue towards London was crowded with supplies destined for the bishop and his party; Geoffrey[1] de Mandeville, who had now again revolted to them, (for formerly, after the capture of the king, he had sworn fidelity to the empress,) and the Londoners, lending every possible assistance, and omitting no circumstance which might distress the empress. The people of Winchester were, though secretly, inclined to her side; regarding the faith they had before pledged to her, although they had been, in some degree, compelled by the bishop to such a measure. In the meanwhile combustibles were hurled from the bishop's castle on the houses of the townspeople, (who, as I have said, rather wished success to the empress than the bishop,) which caught and burnt the whole abbey of nuns, within the city; and the monastery, which is called Hide, without the walls. Here was an image of our crucified Lord, wrought with a profusion of gold and silver and precious stones, through the pious solicitude of Cnut, who was formerly king, and presented it. This being seized by the flames and thrown to the ground, was afterwards stripped of its ornaments at the command of the legate himself: more than five

[1] MS. E. adds from " Geoffrey," to " empress, and."

hundred marks of silver, and thirty of gold, which were found on it, served for a largess to the soldiers. The abbey of nuns at Warewell was also burnt by one William de Ipres, an abandoned character, who feared neither God nor man, because some of the partisans of the empress had secured themselves within it.

§ 51. In the meantime, the earl of Gloucester, though suffering, with his followers, by daily contests with the royalists, and though circumstances turned out far beneath his expectation, yet ever abstained from the burning of churches, notwithstanding he resided in the vicinity of St. Swithun's.   But unable to endure any longer the disgrace of being, together with his party, almost besieged, and seeing fortune inclining towards the enemy, he deemed it expedient to yield to necessity; and, having marshalled his troops, he prepared to depart.   Sending his sister, therefore, and the rest in the vanguard, that she might proceed without interruption, he himself retreated gently, with a chosen few, who had spirit enough not to be alarmed at a multitude.   The earls immediately pursued him, and as he thought it disgraceful and beneath his dignity to fly, and was the chief object of universal attack, he was made captive.   The rest, especially the chiefs, proceeded on their destined journey, and, with the utmost precipitation, reached Devizes.   Thus they departed from Winchester on the day of the Exaltation of the Holy Cross [Sept. 14], which at that time happened on a Sunday, having come thither a few days before the Assumption of the holy mother of God [Aug. 15].   It appeared to some rather miraculous, and was matter of general conversation in England, that the king on the Sunday of the Purification of our Lady [Feb. 2], and the earl on the Sunday of the Exaltation of the life-imparting Cross, should each experience a similar fate.   This, however, was truly worthy of remark and admiration, that no one, on this mischance, ever beheld the earl of Gloucester either dispirited or dejected in countenance ; for he breathed too high a consciousness of dignity, to subject himself to the caprice of fortune; and although he was at first invited by soothing measures, and afterwards assailed by threats, he never consented to treat of his liberation, except with the privity of his sister.   At last the affair was thus decided : that the king and himself should be liberated on equal terms ; no condition being proposed, except that each might defend his party, to the utmost of his abilities, as before.   These matters, after repeated and long discussion, from the Exaltation of the Holy Cross to the festival of All Saints [Sept. 14—Nov. 1], then came to a suitable conclusion ; and on the latter day, the king was released.   On the same day he left his queen, and son, and two of the nobility, at Bristol, as sureties for the liberation of the earl ; and came with the utmost speed to Winchester, where the earl, now brought from Rochester, whither he had first been taken, was at this time confined.   The third day after, when the king came to Winchester, the earl departed, leaving there on that day his son William, as a pledge, till the queen should be released.   Performing with quick despatch the journey to Bristol, he liberated the queen, on whose return, William, the earl's son, was set free.   It is, moreover, sufficiently notorious, that although during the whole of his captivity and of the following months till Christmas, he was enticed, by numberless and magnificent promises, to revolt from his sister, yet he always deemed his fraternal affection of greater importance than any promise which could be made him: for leaving his property and his castles, which he might have quietly enjoyed, he continued unceasingly near the empress at Oxford, where, as I have said before, she fixed her residence and held her court.

§ 52. In the meantime, the legate, a prelate of unbounded spirit, who was never inclined to leave incomplete what he had once purposed, summoned by his legatine authority a council at Westminster, on the octaves of St. Andrew [Dec. 7]. I cannot relate the transactions of this council with that certainty with which I did those of the former, as I was not present. We have heard, that a letter was then read from the sovereign pope, in which he gently rebuked the legate for not endeavouring to release his brother; but that he forgave him his former transgression, and earnestly exhorted him to attempt his liberation by any mode, whether ecclesiastical or secular: that the king himself entered the council, and complained to the reverend assembly, that his own subjects had both made captive, and nearly killed him by the indignities they inflicted on him, who had never refused them justice. That the legate himself, too, with great eloquence, endeavoured to extenuate the odium of his own conduct; saying, that, in truth, he had received the empress, not from inclination, but necessity; for that while his brother's overthrow was yet recent, (all the earls being either dispersed or waiting the issue of events in suspense,) she had surrounded Winchester with her party; that she had obstinately persevered in breaking every promise she had made pertaining to the right of the churches; and that he had it from unquestionable authority, that she and her partisans had not only had designs on his dignity, but even on his life; that, however, God in his mercy had caused matters to fall out contrary to her hopes, so that he himself had escaped destruction, and rescued his brother from captivity; that he commanded, therefore, on the part of God and of the pope, that they should strenuously assist the king, who had been anointed by the will of the people, and with the approbation of the holy see: but that such as disturbed the peace, in favour of the countess of Anjou, should be excommunicated, with the exception of herself, who was sovereign of the Angevins.

§ 53. I do not say, that this speech was kindly received by all the clergy, though certainly no one opposed it; for all the clergy bridled their tongues, either through fear or through reverence. There was one layman sent from the empress, who openly forbade the legate, by the faith which he had pledged to her, to ordain anything, in that council, repugnant to her honour; and said, that he had made oath to the empress not to assist his brother, unless, perchance, by sending him twenty horsemen at the utmost; that her coming to England had been effected by his frequent letters; that her taking the king, and holding him in captivity, had been done principally by his connivance. The advocate affirmed these and many other circumstances, with great harshness of language, and by no means

sparing the legate.   However, he could not be prevailed upon,
by any force of argument, to lay aside his animosity; for, as
I have said before, he was an active perseverer in what he had once
taken in hand.   This year, therefore, (the misfortunes of which
I have briefly related,) was fatal, and nearly destructive to England;
during which, though conceiving that she might now, perhaps,
experience some little respite, yet she became again involved in
calamity, and, unless God's mercy shall shortly come to her relief,
must there long continue.

§ 54. It seems fitting that I should commence the transactions of
this year, which is the year of our Lord one thousand one hundred
and forty-three, with certain events which were unnoticed in the
former; and, at the same time, briefly recapitulate what has been
said, in various places, of Robert earl of Gloucester, son of king
Henry, and submit it, thus arranged, to the consideration of the
reader.   For, as he was the first to espouse the just defence of his
sister, so did he persevere with unshaken constancy in her cause,
without remuneration; I say, without remuneration, because some
of her supporters, either, following the course of fortune, are changed
with its revolutions, or, having already obtained considerable benefits,
fight for justice under expectation of still further recompence:
Robert alone, or nearly alone, uninfluenced by such considerations,
was never swayed, as will appear hereafter, either by hope of advantage or fear of loss.   Let no one, therefore, suspect me of adu-
lation, if I relate these matters circumstantially; for I shall make
no sacrifice to favour; but pure historical truth, without any stain of
falsehood, shall be handed down for the information of posterity.

§ 55. It has been related of the earl, how, first[1] of all the nobility, after David king of Scotland, he confirmed by oath his fealty
to his sister, the empress, for the kingdom of England and the
duchy of Normandy, in the presence of his father Henry: there
having been some contention, as I have said, between him and
Stephen earl of Boulogne, afterwards king of England, who should
swear first; Robert alleging the preference of a son, Stephen the
dignity of a nephew.

§ 56. It has been recorded, too, what reasonable causes, from
December, when his father died, till after the ensuing Easter,
detained him, in Normandy, from coming immediately into England to avenge his sister's injuries: and when at last he did come,
with what just deliberation, and with what proviso, he consented to
do homage to the king; and how justly, in the following year and
thenceforward, he abjured it.

§ 57. Nor has his second arrival in England from Normandy,
after his father's death, with his sister, been omitted; where, relying on the favour of God and his innate courage, he ventured
himself, as into a desert full of wild beasts, though scarcely accompanied by one hundred and forty horsemen.   Neither has it been
unnoticed, that, amid such tumult of war, while anxious watch was
kept on all sides, he boldly came to Bristol with only twelve horse-

---

[1] This seems an oversight: as he had before related, more than once, that
Stephen preceded Robert in taking the oath to Matilda.

men, having committed his sister to safe custody, as he supposed, at
Arundel; nor with what prudence, at that time, he received her from
the very midst of her enemies, and afterwards advanced her in all
things to the utmost of his power ; ever busied on her account, and
neglecting his own interest to secure hers, while some persons,
taking advantage of his absence, plundered his possessions on every
side ; and, lastly, urged by what necessity, namely, to rescue his
son-in-law, whom the king had besieged, he engaged in an hazardous
conflict, and took the king prisoner. This fortunate event, however,
was somewhat obscured by his own capture at Winchester, as I
have recorded in the transactions of the former year ; though, by
the grace of God, he showed himself, not so much an object or
commiseration, as of praise, in that capture. For, when he saw
that the royalist earls were so persevering in the pursuit that the
business could not be gotten through without loss on his part, he
sent forward all those for whom he was under apprehension, and
more especially the empress. When they had proceeded far
enough to escape in safety, he followed leisurely, that the retreat
might not resemble a flight, and received the attack of the pur-
suers himself ; thus purchasing, by his own detention, the liberty of
his friends. And now even at the moment of his capture, no one,
as I have said above, perceived him either dispirited, or humbled
in language ; he seemed so far to tower above fortune, that he
compelled his persecutors, for I am loth to call them enemies, to
respect him. Wherefore the queen, though she might have
remembered that her husband had been fettered by his command,
yet never suffered fetters of any kind to be put upon him, nor pre-
sumed on her dignity to treat him dishonourably. And finally, at
Rochester, for thither he was conducted, he went freely whither he
pleased to the churches below the castle, and conversed with whom
he chose, the queen only being present : after her departure he was
held in free custody in the keep, and such forethought and sense of
security had he, that, getting money from his vassals in Kent, he
bought some valuable horses, which were both serviceable and
beneficial to him afterwards.

§ 58. The earls, and those whose business it was to speak of
such matters, at first, tried if he would allow of the king and himself being liberated on equal terms. Though his countess, Mabil,
out of solicitude for her beloved husband, would have embraced
these terms the moment she heard them, being, through conjugal
affection, bent on his liberation, yet he, in his wiser policy, refused ;
asserting that a king and an earl were not of equal importance ;
however, if they would allow all who had been taken with him, or
for him, to be set at liberty, to this he might consent. But the
earls and other royalists would not assent to these terms ; they
were anxious, indeed, for the king's liberty, but not at their own
pecuniary loss ; for earl Gilbert had taken William of Salisbury ;
and William de Ipres had taken Humphry de Bohun ; and others
had made such captures as they could, at Winchester, greedily
expecting large sums for their ransom.

§ 59. Next attacking the earl another way, they anxiously endea-

voured to seduce him with magnificent promises. Would he go
over to the king's side, and dismiss his sister, he should govern the
whole country; all things should await his decision; the crown
should be the only distinction between him and the king; over all
others he should rule as he pleased. The earl rejected these unbounded promises, with a memorable reply, which I wish posterity
to hear and to admire. " I am not my own master," said he,
" but am in another's power; when I shall see myself at my own
disposal, I promise to do everything which reason dictates on the
matter you propound."

§ 60. Irritated and incensed at this, when they could do nothing
by fair means, they began to threaten that they would send him
over sea to Boulogne, and keep him in perpetual bondage till
death. Still, however, with a serene countenance, dispelling their
threats, he firmly and truly protested that he feared nothing
less: for he relied on the spirit of the countess, his wife, and the
courage of his partisans, who would immediately send the king
into Ireland, if they heard of any foul deed perpetrated against
himself.

§ 61. A month elapsed in these transactions; so difficult a
work was it to effect the liberation of princes whom fortune had
fettered with her chain. But, at length, the supporters of the
empress having conferred together, entreated the earl by frequent
messages, that as he could not do what he would, according to
the comic writer, he would do what he could; that he should
allow, therefore, the king and himself to be set at liberty on
equal terms. " Otherwise," said they, " we fear lest the earls,
inspirited by the consciousness of their great and most distinguished exploit in making you captive, should attack us one by
one, reduce our castles, and even make an attempt upon your
sister."

§ 62. Robert, wrought upon at length, assented to the proposal
of the legate and archbishop, but still on condition that none of the
castles, or territories, should be restored, which had come under
the power of the empress, or of any of her adherents, since the capture of the king; but he could not by any means obtain the release
of his friends, as he had given offence to some persons in rejecting,
with a kind of superciliousness, their magnificent promises with
respect to the government of the whole kingdom. And as they
were extremely anxious that, for the royal dignity, the king should
be first set at liberty, and then the earl; when he demurred to this,
the legate and the archbishop made oath, that if the king, after his
own liberation, refused to release the earl, they would forthwith
deliver themselves up into Robert's power, to be conducted
wherever he pleased.

§ 63. Nor did he rest here; for his sagacious mind discovered
an additional security. It might fall out, that the king, as often
happens, listening to evil counsel, would consider the detention of
his brother and of the archbishop as of very little consequence, so
that he himself were at his ease. He demanded, therefore, from

them both, separately, instruments, with their seals, addressed to the pope, to the following effect : " That the sovereign pope was to understand, that they, for the liberation of the king and the peace of the kingdom, had bound themselves to the earl by this covenant, that, if the king refused to liberate him after his own release, they themselves would willingly surrender to his custody. Should it, therefore, come to this calamitous issue, they earnestly entreated, (what it would well become the papal goodness voluntarily to perform,) that he would release them, who were his suffragans, as well as the earl, from unjustifiable durance." There was something more to the same effect.

§ 64. These writings, received from both prelates, Robert deposited in a place of safety, and came to Winchester with them and a great company of the barons. The king also, as has been before observed, coming thither soon after, had a friendly interview with the earl. But although he, and all the earls present, eagerly busied themselves in bringing over Robert to their wishes, yet, " firm as a rock amid the ocean in his resistance," he rendered their attempts abortive, or refuted them by argument. He affirmed, that it was neither reasonable nor natural, that he should desert his sister, whose cause he had justly espoused, not for any benefit to himself, nor so much out of dislike to the king, as regard to his oath, which, they also ought to remember, it was impiety to violate; especially when he called to mind, that he had been enjoined by the pope to respect the oath he had taken to his sister in the presence of his father. Thus failing of peace, they severally departed.

§ 65. The reason why I have not incorporated these events with the transactions of the former year, is, that I did not then know them ; for I have always dreaded to transmit anything to posterity, through my narrative, the truth of which I could not perfectly vouch for. What, then, I have to relate of the present year, will commence as follows :

§ 66. The respective parties of the empress and of the king conducted themselves with quiet forbearance from Christmas to Lent [March 4], anxious rather to preserve their own, than to ravage the possessions of others. The king went to a distant part of the kingdom, for the purpose of quelling some disturbances. Lent coming on, gave all a respite from war ; in the midst of which, the empress came with her party to Devizes, where her secret designs were debated. So much of them however transpired, that it was known that all her partisans had agreed to send for the earl of Anjou, who was most interested in the defence of the inheritance of his wife and children in England. Men of respectability were, therefore, despatched, and such as might fitly execute a business of such magnitude.

§ 67. Not long after, in the Easter holidays, the king, while meditating, as it is said, some harsh measures, was detained by an acute disease at Northampton ; so severe, indeed, that he was reported, almost throughout England, as being at the point of death.

His sickness continued till after Pentecost [June 7], when returning health gradually restored him.

§ 68. In the meantime, the messengers returning from Anjou, related the result of their mission to the empress and the princes in a second council, held at Devizes on the octaves of Pentecost [June 14]. They said, that the earl of Anjou, in some measure, favoured the mission of the nobility; but that among them all, he was only well acquainted with the earl of Gloucester, of whose prudence and fidelity, greatness of mind and industry, he had long since had proof. Were he to make a voyage to him, he would, as far as he was able, accede to his wishes; but that all other persons would expend their labour in passing and re-passing to no purpose.

§ 69. The hopes of all the assembly being thus excited, they entreated that the earl would condescend to undertake this task, on account of the inheritance of his sister and nephews. At first he excused himself, alleging the difficulty of the business; the perilous journey, beset with enemies, on either side of the sea; that it would be attended with danger to his sister; as, in his absence, those persons would be hardly able to defend her, who, distrusting even the strength of their own party, had nearly deserted her during his captivity. Yielding at length to the general desire, he demanded hostages, especially from those who were considered as the chief persons, to be taken with him into Normandy, and to be pledges, as well to the earl of Anjou, as to the empress; and that all, continuing at Oxford, should unite in defending her from injury to the utmost while he was absent. His propositions were eagerly approved, and hostages given him to be conducted into Normandy.

§ 70. Robert, therefore, bidding adieu to his sister, and taking with him his hostages and some light troops, proceeded by safe marches to Wareham, which town and castle he had, long since, entrusted to his eldest son, William. There, soon after the festival of St. John [June 24], committing himself, by the grace of God, to the ocean, with such vessels as he then possessed, he weighed anchor. When they were about mid-sea, a tempest arose, and all, except two, were dispersed; some were driven back, and some carried beyond their destination: two only, in one of which was the earl with his most faithful adherents, keeping their course, arrived in the wished for port. Proceeding thus to Caen, he sent messengers for the earl of Anjou. The earl came without reluctance, but stated his difficulties, and those not a few, to the object of the embassy, when proposed to him; among others, that he should be detained from coming into England by the rebellion of many castles in Normandy. This circumstance delayed the earl of Gloucester's return longer than he had intended: for, that he might deprive the earl of Anjou of every excuse, he assisted him in subduing ten castles in Normandy, the[1] names of which were, Tenerchebrei, Seithilaret, Bri-

---

[1] To the end of the sentence from E.

.chesart, Alani, Bastonborg, Triveres, Castel de Vira, Plaseiz, Vilers, Moretoin.   Yet, even by this activity, he furthered the end of his mission but little.   The earl of Anjou stated fresh causes, as the former were done away, to excuse his coming into England.   Indeed, as a very singular favour, he permitted his eldest son, by the empress, to accompany his uncle to England, by whose presence the chiefs might be encouraged to defend the cause of the lawful heir.   The youth is named Henry, after his grandfather; may he hereafter resemble him in happiness and in power.

§ 71. In England, in the meantime, the king, seizing the opportunity of the earl's absence, came unexpectedly to Wareham, and finding it slightly garrisoned, he burnt and plundered the town, and immediately got possession of the castle also.   Not content with this (as he saw fortune inclined to favour him), three days before the festival of St. Michael, by an unexpected[1] chance, he burnt the city of Oxford, and laid siege to the castle, in which was the empress with her household troops.   This he did with such determined resolution, that he declared no hope of advantage or fear of loss should induce him to depart, till the castle was delivered up, and the empress surrendered to his power.   Shortly after, all the nobility of the empress's party, ashamed at being absent from their sovereign in violation of their compact, assembled in large bodies at Wallingford, with the determination of attacking the king, if he would risk a battle in the open plain; but they had no intention of assailing him within the city, as the earl of Gloucester had so fortified it with ditches that it appeared impregnable, unless by fire.

§ 72. These rumours becoming prevalent in Normandy, Robert earl of Gloucester hastened his return.   He embarked, therefore, somewhat more than three hundred horsemen on board fifty-two vessels; to these were added two which he took at sea on his return.   God's grace so singularly favoured his pious resolution, that not one ship out of so great a number was separated, but all nearly close together, or gently proceeding one before the other, ploughed the calm bosom of the deep.   Nor did the waves violently dash against the fleet, but rather seemed subserviently to further their passage; like that most beautiful appearance of the sea, when the wave, gradually approaching, gently breaks upon the shore.   Thus making the port of Wareham, these favoured vessels restored the earl and all his companions to the wishes of their friends.

§ 73. He had, at first, thought of landing at Southampton, at once to wreak his vengeance, both on its inhabitants and on their lord; but this resolution was changed through the repeated entreaties of the Vituli, who were fearful that their dearest connexions, who resided at Southampton, would be involved in the general calamity. These are a kind of mariners, who are known by the name of

[1] The garrison having sallied out against him, he suddenly passed a ford, which was not generally known, and repelling the enemy, entered the town with them. Gesta Regis Stephani, 958.

Vituli; and as they are his faithful adherents, he thought fit to listen to their petitions, and desist from his design. Again, it appeared more dignified to return to the place whence he had departed, and to recover by force what he had lost by a similar mode. Reducing, therefore, immediately the port and town, he laid siege to the castle; which by its strength stimulated the spirit, not to call it obstinacy, of the king's choicest troops who defended it. Yet, nevertheless, soon after, the garrison, shaken in their resolution by the engines of the earl, and greatly alarmed, begged a truce, that, as is the custom of the military, they might demand assistance from the king; consenting to deliver up the castle, if he refused to come by a certain day. This, though he was possessed with the utmost impatience to become master of the fortress, was very agreeable to the earl, as it led him to suppose it might draw off Stephen from besieging his sister. We may imagine what firmness of mind this man possessed, who, with little more than three hundred horsemen, and, as yet, joined by no succours in England, could undauntedly await the king, who was reported to have more than a thousand; for many persons had joined the siege, not so much through dislike to the empress, as through the hope of plunder.

§ 74. However, when it was certified that the king refused assistance to the besieged at Wareham, the earl, pertinaciously keeping up the attack, got possession of the castle, and with the same celerity subdued the island of Portland, which they had fortified, as well as a third castle, called Lulleworth, which belonged to a certain chamberlain, called William of Glastonbury, who had lately revolted from the empress. Robert, then, at the beginning of Advent [Nov. 29], summoned the whole of Matilda's partisans to Cirencester: where, all resolving to afford their sovereign every possible assistance, they meditated a march to Oxford, courageously determining to give the king battle, unless he retreated. But as they were on their route, the pleasing account reached them, that the empress had escaped from the blockaded castle at Oxford, and was now at Wallingford in security. Turning aside thither, then, at the suggestion of their sovereign, (since the soldiers who had remained at her departure, after delivering up the castle, had gone away without molestation, and the holidays admonished them to repose awhile,) they resolved to abstain from battle, and retired to their homes.

HERE ENDS THE THIRD BOOK OF MALMESBURY'S HISTORY OF HIS OWN TIMES.

§ 75. I would very willingly subjoin the manner of the empress's liberation, did I know it to a certainty; for it is undoubtedly one of God's manifest miracles. This, however, is sufficiently notorious, that, through fear of the earl's approach, many of the besiegers at Oxford stole away, wherever they were able, and the rest remitted

their vigilance, and kept not so good a look-out as before ; more
anxious for their own safety, in case it came to a battle, than bent
on the destruction of others.[1]

But these matters, with God's permission, shall be more largely
treated in the following volume.

[1] Some MSS. (C. D. G. K. L 2.) after "others" read, "This circumstance being
remarked by the townsmen, the empress, with only four soldiers, made her escape
through a small postern, and passed the river. Afterwards, as necessity sometimes, and indeed almost always, discovers means and ministers courage, she
went to Abingdon on foot, and thence reached Wallingford on horseback. But
this I purpose describing more fully, if, by God's permission, I shall ever learn
the truth of it from those who were present :"—and omit "But these matters, &c."

THE ACTS OF KING STEPHEN, AND THE BATTLE OF THE STANDARD.

HERE BEGINS THE HISTORY OF RICHARD, PRIOR OF THE CHURCH OF HEXHAM, OF PIOUS MEMORY, CONCERNING THE ACTS OF KING STEPHEN, AND THE BATTLE OF THE STANDARD.

A. D. 1135. IN the year of the incarnate Word 1135, sixty-nine years after the invasion of England by the Normans, Henry, king of England, in the sixty-eighth year of his age, was seized with illness, occasioned by eating some lampreys, and died at St. Denis, in a forest of Normandy called Leuns, on Monday, the fourth of the nones of December [2d Dec.]. He had an illustrious reign of thirty-five years and four months. His body, in compliance with his own directions, was conveyed to England, and buried at Reading. Justice and peace, which had so long ruled with him, perished in like manner with him both in Normandy and England ; and the defence of justice (which at that time everywhere held sole rule) being removed, in the place of peace and justice, violence and rapine, slaughter and devastation, unheard-of cruelties and endless calamities, tyrannized far and wide. After his death all these evils raged the more freely and fiercely, in proportion to the stern force and strict justice by which in his lifetime so many had been overthrown, kept under, despoiled, disinherited, and exiled. Seizing from this event the opportunity so ardently longed for, each one hastened to avenge himself whilst it lay in his power, to effect whatever mischief he could. At this period William, surnamed Transversus, who by a grant from king Henry held the lordship of Pontefract, (as the town is called,) having received at that place a mortal wound from a knight named Pain, died three days afterwards, having assumed the monastic habit. Then Ilbert de Lacy, the son, regained the lordship of which king Henry had deprived his father, Robert de Lacy ; and many similar cases occurred at that time throughout England and Normandy. In his youth the noble king Henry was distinguished for his honourable bearing; he had frequently undergone the trial of adverse circumstances, and was well practised in martial conflicts. He was a man of counsel and foresight, sagacity and prudence, firm in mind, courageous in spirit, truthful in speech, faithful to his promises, resolute in his threats, steadfast in friendship, persistent in hatred, patient in adversity, moderate in prosperity, fluent in oratory, stern in justice, equitable in judgment, a bitter foe to his opponents, a warm friend to his allies. Having, on the death of his brother William, acquired the throne of England, he (by marvellous cunning) obtained from his brother, earl Robert, the dukedom of Normandy, and managed the affairs of both states with great ability, and, with a policy which cannot be described, he gained the ascendency over all who were unfavourable to him. He put down many men of high rank on account of their bad faith, and loaded with high honours many of humble birth who proved honest and loyal to him. He also revived the good laws[1] and customs of his predecessor and relative, king Edward; and when they were amended, as he saw fit, by his wisdom, and confirmed by his authority, he caused them to be strictly and constantly observed by rich as well as poor throughout his kingdom. Moreover, he visited with severe punishment thieves and robbers, plunderers and evil-doers, forgers of base coin, and wild prodigals. Thus in his days was a bright season of peace, and many monasteries were changed to the profession of monks, and especially of the regular canons, where previously there had been none. He indeed founded, and with regal munificence endowed, two convents, one of monks at Reading, where he desired to be buried, and the other of canons at Cirencester, and appointed to both abbots of their respective orders. The monastery at Reading he favoured with his patronage, and in a conspicuous place he built a church of very beautiful workmanship, and furnished it with princely revenues, and a numerous choir of monks. The convent of Cirencester he founded four years before his death, and established there regular canons, whom he provided with abundant supplies. He was distinguished for his admirable bounty and due regard towards religious and poor. None of his successors so strongly prohibited as he unjust extortions in the realm, or so skilfully disposed all to quiet subjection and orderly behaviour; none so piously regarded the clergy, or provided with such sumptuous beneficence for the poor and needy.

He had two queens; the first, named Matilda, was a daughter of Malcolm, king of Scotland, and by her he had one daughter, who married first the emperor Henry of Germany, and afterwards Geoffrey, earl of Anjou. By this queen he had also one son, called William, who perished at sea, with the principal nobility of England and Normandy. After the death of Matilda he married a second queen, named Adeliza, the daughter of Godfrey, duke of Lovaine, by whom he had no issue. But, through fornication and adultery, he had several children; for these two vices, sensuality and covetousness, had too much the rule over him, and hence many were depraved by his bad example. Being in Normandy a little before his death, he partook of some lampreys, which speedily brought on an illness of which he died, as was before stated. On his demise, immediately there arose wicked men and sinners, setting at nought all the rules of justice and of order, and fiercely giving themselves up to devastations and slaughters, incendiarism and every other form of crime. For (as we have said), in the commencement of his reign, he had given the people just laws and liberties,

---

[1] See the "Leges regis Henrici primi," in Thorpe's Ancient Laws of England, i. 497.

established them by charter, confirmed them by his seal, and directed them to be laid up in his treasury at Winchester, as the following document will clearly show :—

" Henry,[1] by the grace of God, king of the English, to all his faithful people, whether French-born or English, throughout all England, wisheth greeting.

" Know ye that by the mercy of God, and the united will of the barons of the kingdom of England, I have been crowned king of this realm.   And forasmuch as the kingdom has been oppressed by unjust extortions, I, from reverence to God and the love which I bear towards you all, in the first place, acknowledge the freedom of God's holy church; so that I will neither sell it, nor let it out to farm, nor on the death of an archbishop, bishop, or abbot, will I receive anything from the domain, or from the vassals of the church, until his successor shall be installed.   And I hereby abolish all the evil practices by which the kingdom of England has been unrighteously oppressed, and some of those evil practices I here specify.   If any of my barons, or earls, or others who hold under me shall die, his heir shall not redeem his land, as the practice was in the time of my brother, but shall relieve it by a just and legal payment.   And in like manner the vassals of my barons shall relieve their lands from their lords by a just and legal payment.   And if any of my barons or other vassals shall desire to give in marriage his daughter, sister, niece, or other relative, he shall consult me thereupon ; but neither will I receive anything from him for this permission, nor will I prevent him from bestowing her in marriage, unless he desire to unite her to my enemy.   And if, on the death of a baron or other vassal, a daughter shall be left an heiress, I will bestow her with her possessions by the advice of my barons.   And if, on the death of a husband, his wife shall be left without children, she shall have her dowry and her marriage settlement, and I will not give her in marriage without her own consent ; but if the wife be left with children, she shall have her dowry and her marriage settlement while she keeps her body in due order, and I will not give her in marriage without her own consent ; and either the wife, or other of the relatives to whom it justly pertains, shall be the guardian of the children's property.   And I order my barons to act in a similar manner to the sons, or daughters, or wives of their vassals.   From henceforth I utterly prohibit the common coinage of money, which was taken throughout the cities and counties, which was not in the time of king Edward ; and if any one, either coiner or other, be apprehended with base coin, let strict justice be done upon him.   I remit all the pleas and the debts which were owing to my brother, excepting only my legal farms, and excepting those which were contracted for the inheritances of others, or for those properties which of right pertained to others.   And if any one had made an agreement for his own inheritance, I remit that and all those reliefs which were contracted for rightful inheritances.   And if any of my barons or vassals shall fall sick, in whatsoever manner he

_____
[1] Collated with the copy extant in the work cited in the last note, p. 497.

shall grant or by will dispose of his property, I confirm the deed.
But if dying suddenly by violence or sickness, he shall not grant or
dispose of his property, his wife, or his children, or his relatives
and lawful vassals, shall divide it for the good of his soul, as to
them shall seem best. But if he shall have been convicted of
treason or crime, he shall thus make satisfaction. If any of my
barons or vassals shall become amenable to the law, he shall not
give security of his money at the will of his lord, as he did in
the time of my father and brother, but he shall make satisfaction
according to the nature of his crime, as satisfaction was made
before my father's time, in the days of my other predecessors. All
murders perpetrated before the day of my coronation I pardon; and
all which shall be henceforward committed, shall be legally atoned
for according to the law of king Edward. The forests, by the
united consent of my barons, I retain in my own hand, as my
father held them. To knights who do military service for their
lands, I, by my own gift, grant the lands of their own domains to
be free from all tribute and work; so that being freed from so heavy
a burden, they may so fully equip themselves with horses and arms,
as to be ready and prepared for my service and the defence of my
kingdom. I establish a firm peace in the whole of my kingdom,
and order it to be henceforth kept. I grant you the law of king
Edward, with the amendments made by my father with the advice
of his barons. If any one since the death of my brother William
has taken anything from me, or from the property of another, the
whole shall be immediately restored without a fine; but if any
one after this shall retain any such property, he in whose possession it is found shall make heavy satisfaction to me.

" These are the witnesses hereof: Maurice,[1] bishop of London,
William, bishop-elect of Winchester, Gerard, bishop of Hereford,
earl Henry, earl Simon, earl Walter Giffard, R. de Mountford,
Eudo the butler, and Roger Bigot. Farewell."

Let what has been thus briefly told concerning him suffice for
the present. If any one desires to know his acts more at length,
and how he conducted himself in his kingdom, he may find it in
the histories of the transactions of the English. Henry was succeeded in his throne by Stephen, earl of Boulogne, his nephew, by
his sister the countess of Blois, and the brother of earl Theobald.

A.D. 1136. Stephen, earl of Boulogne, being chosen by the nobles
of the kingdom, with the sanction of the clergy and people, was
crowned king at London on Christmas-day, by William, archbishop
of Canterbury. The beginning and course of his reign was overwhelmed with so many and so violent discordant commotions, that
how to describe them, or what may be their termination, no one
can yet know. The king himself, however, although straitened on
every side by calamities numberless and extreme, preserved ever a
firm courage and a cheerful countenance; and, as if already sure
of ultimate victory, smiled at the threats and endeavours of his
foes, the artifices of the designing, the perfidy of traitors, and the

[1] At this point there is a considerable variation among the several MS. copies.
See Thorpe, p. 502.

loss of worldly possessions, however great, as if he did not feel them, or counted them for nothing. This confidence and assurance on his part filled his enemies with amazement and confusion, but inspired his friends with energy, boldness, and comfort. He was a man also of so much kindness and good nature, that his very enemies were attracted to his side, and experienced from him a degree of kindness beyond their expectation. From this cause he succeeded in levying large masses of subsidiary troops, by means of whom he effected his objects in Normandy and England. For Geoffrey, earl of Anjou, (who had married king Henry's daughter, the empress, as she was called after her marriage with the emperor,) to whose son England and Normandy had been assigned by oath, so soon as he was aware that Stephen was chosen king, devastated and laid waste many districts, and took and maintained, in opposition to him, many fortresses in Normandy. Likewise also died David, king of Scotland, the uncle of the same lady, who, about Christmas, seized and held with a strong force five towns in the province of Northumbria; to wit, Lugubalia, called in English Carlisle, Carrum, by the English called Wark, Alnwick, Norham, and Newcastle; but he altogether failed to take Bambrough. He received from the chiefs and nobles of that locality vows and pledges of fidelity to his niece, the empress. It was his design to attack Durham also, but king Stephen with a large force arrived there on Ash-Wednesday (which that year fell on the nones of February) [5th Feb.], and remained there fifteen days. At length a conference was held in that province, and a treaty being concluded between the two kings, Henry, son of David, king of Scotland, did homage to king Stephen at York. With his father's earldom of Huntingdon the king gave him Carlisle and Doncaster, with all their appurtenances; and according to the account of some, who state that they were present at that convention, he promised him that if he purposed to bestow upon any one the earldom of Northumberland, he would first cause the claim which Henry, son of the king of Scotland, might have upon it, to be fairly adjudicated in his court. King David restored to Stephen, king of England, four of the aforesaid castles which he had seized; for the fifth, namely, Carlisle, had been ceded to him, an agreement with pledges being concluded by the subjects on each side. At the Easter following [22d March], Henry, son of the king of Scotland, was present at the court which Stephen, king of England, held in state at London, being there received with the highest honours, and placed at table on the king's right hand. On account of this, William, archbishop of Canterbury, withdrew from court, and some of the nobles of England, enraged at the king, gave vent to their disapprobation in the presence of Henry himself. David, king of Scotland, was highly indignant at this, and on his son's return, refused to allow him again to visit the king's court, though frequently invited.

In this year the Welsh ravaged a great portion of the land of Stephen, king of England, and cut off by stratagem in their country two of his barons, Richard Fitz-Roger and Pain Fitz-John;

they afterwards, however, made peace with him. In the same year, also, Baldwin de Redvers, disappointed at not obtaining a barony which the king had promised him, fortified against him his town of Exeter; but the king laid his land waste, and after a lengthened siege took the town by storm, and having made him prisoner, banished him from England and Normandy; he took refuge, however, with Geoffrey, earl of Anjou, and his wife the empress.

In this year also, Innocent, pontiff of the see of Rome, sent to Stephen, king of England, a letter, in which he confirmed him by apostolic authority in the sovereignty of England. The following is a copy:—

"Innocent, bishop, the servant of the servants of God, to his well-beloved son in Christ, the illustrious Stephen, king of the English, health and the apostolic benediction.

"The King of kings and Lord of lords, in whose hand are all the powers and rights of all kingdoms, in the unfathomable dispensation of his divine providence, changes times and transfers kingdoms at his will, as saith the prophet, 'The Most High God ruleth in the kingdom of men, and appointeth over it whomsoever He will.' [Dan. iv. 17.] What blessings, what happy tranquillity, what just severity, abounded in the kingdom of England and dukedom of Normandy, under the rule of our son of glorious memory, king Henry, have been made clearly evident since he has been removed from earthly concerns. For being a favourer of religious men, a lover of peace and justice, a kind comforter of widows and orphans, a defender of those who were powerless to defend themselves, since his decease (as we have been informed) religion has been unsettled in the kingdom of England, no law enforcing peace or justice has been available for the king's assistance, and impunity has attended the most atrocious crimes. But, in order that such dire ferocity may not continue to swell and rage against God's people, the mercy of divine love has listened to the prayers of the religious, and mightily set itself against such enormities; and has therefore brought it to pass, that by the united voice and common consent both of nobles and people, you should be chosen king, and consecrated by the primates of the kingdom, as is certified to us by the letters of our venerable brethren, the archbishops and bishops of those parts, and of those lovers of the holy Roman church, the renowned king of the French and the illustrious count Theobald, as well as by the declaration of trustworthy men. Knowing that in your person the divine favour accords with the choice of men so worthy, and knowing also that for the recompence of a sure hope on the day of your consecration, you vowed obedience and reverence to St. Peter; and since you are known to be descended almost in a direct line from the royal lineage of the aforesaid kingdom, we, satisfied with what has been done in your case, receive you with fatherly affection, as a favoured son of St. Peter and of the holy Roman church, and heartily desire to retain you in the same privilege of regard and intimacy by which your predecessor of illustrious memory was by us distinguished."

King Stephen, by these and other means, being established on the throne of England, convoked by royal proclamation an assembly of the bishops and nobles, and in conjunction with them enacted as follows :—

" I Stephen, by the grace of God, chosen king of England by the consent of the clergy and people, having been consecrated by William, archbishop of Canterbury, legate of the holy Roman church, and confirmed by Innocent, pontiff of the holy Roman see, do from reverence and love of God acknowledge the liberty of holy church, and vow due respect to it.   I promise that in the church or ecclesiastical matters, I will do or allow nothing of a simoniacal nature.   I allow and maintain that the judgment and control of ecclesiastical persons and all the clergy, and the patronage of ecclesiastical benefices, is in the power of the bishops.   I grant and ordain that the rights of churches confirmed by their charter, and their customs used by ancient tenure, shall remain inviolate.   All the estates of churches, and the tenures which they held on the day of the decease of my grandfather, king William, I grant without bond or restriction, and exempt from all litigious claims.   But if there shall still remain anything held or possessed before the death of that king now wanting to the church, I reserve the restitution or discussion of the same to my own pleasure and arbitration.   I confirm whatever has been derived by them from the liberality of kings, the bounty of nobles, the oblation, conveyance, or transference of the faithful, since the demise of that king. I promise that in all things I will pursue peace and justice, and by all means in my power secure their continuance.   I reserve to myself the forests which my grandfather William, and my uncle William the Second, made and held ; but all the others, which were added by king Henry, I yield and restore without cavil to the churches and kingdom. If any bishop, abbot, or other ecclesiastic, shall before his death assign or bequeath his property in a reasonable manner, I grant a confirmation of the act ; but if he shall be cut off by sudden death, it shall be assigned as the church may advise for the good of his soul.   While any sees are vacant of their proper pastors, they and all their possessions shall be entrusted to the management and charge of the clergy, or approved men of that church, until a pastor be canonically appointed. I totally prohibit all extortions, injustice, and false actions, wrongfully effected either by sheriffs or others.   I will observe good laws and ancient and right customs in the hundreds, and in pleas and other legal processes, and order and decree that they shall be observed.   All these things I grant and confirm, saving my royal and lawful dignity.

" The witnesses hereto are, William, archbishop of Canterbury, Hugh, archbishop of Rouen, Henry, bishop of Winchester, Roger, bishop of Salisbury, Alexander, bishop of Lincoln, Nigel, bishop of Ely, Herbert, bishop of Norwich, Simon, bishop of Worcester, Bernard, bishop of St. David's, Audoenus, bishop of Evreux, Richard, bishop of Avranches, Robert, bishop of Hereford, John, bishop of Rochester, Adelwulf, bishop of Carlisle, Roger the chancellor, Henry the king's nephew, Robert, earl of Gloucester,

William, earl of Warren, Ralph, earl of Chester, Roger, earl of
Warwick, Robert de Vere, Milo de Gloucester, Robert de Olli,
Brian, son of the earl-constable, William Martel, Hugh Bigot,
Humfrey de Bohun, Simon de Beauchamp, the seneschals, William
de Albini, Martel de Albini, the cup-bearers, Robert de Ferrers,
William Peverel, Simon de Senlis, William de Albania, Hugh de St.
Clair, Ilbert de Lacy. Dated at Oxford, in the year of our Lord one
thousand one hundred and thirty-six, and the first of my reign."

By these and other methods, Stephen being speedily settled in
the kingdom of England, gave and granted (in the first year of his
reign) laws and customs of this nature to his realm, and faithfully
promised that he and his followers would most strictly observe
them. In the same year, in the month of August, king Stephen
crossed into Normandy, on account of the war with the earl of
Anjou. William, archbishop of Canterbury, died in the month of
November, and was buried in his own city.

A.D. 1137. In the following year, immediately after Easter
[11th April], when king David had levied his troops, he set out to
lay waste Northumberland, in violation of the treaty of peace.
But at the command of king Stephen, (who still remained in Normandy,) the greater part of the earls and barons of England, with
a large force of soldiers, marched to Newcastle in Northumberland,
being prepared to offer resistance should he invade England. At
length, by means of envoys, a suspension of arms was agreed upon
until the following Advent [28th Nov.], and after forty days they
retired to their own quarters. On king Stephen's return from Normandy in Advent, after having, on payment of a large sum, concluded a two years' truce with the earl of Anjou, the ambassadors
of David, king of Scotland, and his son Henry, speedily presented
themselves, holding out a withdrawal of the armistice unless he
would confer on Henry the earldom of Northumberland, but the
king gave no ear to their demand.

A.D. 1138. On the fourth ides of January [10th Jan.], king
David's nephew William, son of Duncan, with a portion of David's
army, made a nocturnal attack upon the fortress called Carrum, in
the king of England's territory, and having plundered the neighbourhood around, proceeded to storm the castle. Afterwards the
king himself and his son Henry arrived with a further reinforcement,
and applying the whole strength of their resources, attempted to
carry the town by various assaults with battering machines and
other implements, and after that laid siege to it for three weeks.
Yet he gained no advantage, but, on the contrary, every attempt
proved injurious to himself : for the knights and others who were
in the fortress, most ably defending themselves and the town, killed
his standard-bearer and many others of his men, under his own
eyes, and wounded many more. The king, perceiving the inutility
of his efforts, and the many and daily increasing losses to himself
and his troops, at length raised the siege, and rushed with his
whole force to devastate Northumberland. And then that execrable army, more atrocious than the whole race of pagans, neither
fearing God nor regarding man, spread desolation over the whole

province, and murdered everywhere persons of both sexes, of every age and rank, and overthrew, plundered, and burned towns, churches, and houses. For the sick on their couches, women pregnant and in childbed, infants in the womb, innocents at the breast, or on the mother's knee, with the mothers themselves, decrepit old men and worn-out old women, and persons debilitated from whatever cause, wherever they met with them, they put to the edge of the sword, and transfixed with their spears; and by how much more horrible a death they could despatch them, so much the more did they rejoice. The mournful lamentation of the Psalmist then plainly received its fulfilment, "O God, the heathen are come into thine inheritance. Thy holy temple have they defiled, and made Jerusalem an heap of stones," (Ps. lxxix. 1,) and, indeed, the whole remaining portion of that psalm. It is said that in one place they slew a multitude of children together, and having collected their blood into a brook which they had previously dammed back, they drank the mixture, of which the greater part was pure blood. It is said, also, that in the church they shattered the crucifixes with every mark of dishonour, in contempt of Christ and to their own infamy; they dug up the altars, and near them, yea, upon them, they slaughtered the clergy and the innocent children. Wherefore we may again not unfitly exclaim in lamentation with the Prophet, "O God, Thou hast cast us out, and scattered us abroad: Thou hast also been displeased, and hast not turned unto us again," (Ps. lx.) and so on as there follows. That infamous army received accessions from the Normans, Germans, and English, from the Northumbrians and Cumbrians, from Teviotdale and Lothian, from the Picts, commonly called Galwegians, and the Scots, and no one knew their number; for multitudes uncalled-for allied themselves with those above mentioned, either from love of plunder, or opportunity of revenge, or the mere desire of mischief with which that region was rife. Overrunning the province, and sparing none, they ravaged with sword and fire almost all Northumberland as far as the river Tyne, excepting the towns and the sea-coast which lies on the eastern side, but this they designed to devastate on their return. A portion of that army also crossed the Tyne, and massacred numberless persons in the wilds, laying waste in the same way the greater part of the territory of St. Cuthbert on the west side.

While these things were being perpetrated by his followers, the king of Scotland with a considerable force occupied Corbridge. At this period a monastery[1] of the Cistercian rule, founded the same year on the property of Ralph de Merley, was destroyed, and very many others were overwhelmed with the heaviest afflictions. Wherefore the monastery at the mouth of the river Tyne, called in English Tynemouth, in order to secure itself and its inmates in this urgent need, paid to the king of Scotland and his men twenty-seven marks of silver. In this raging and tempestuous period, that noble monastery of Hexham, (although in the very midst of the collision, and placed as it were on the very route of these ruffians,

[1] Namely, Newminster, near Morpeth. See p. 12.

so as to be surrounded by them on every side,) yet on account of the renowned merits of its tutelary saints, Andrew the apostle, and Wilfrid, bishop and martyr, and of its other patrons, Saints Acca, Alcmund, and Eata, bishops and confessors, and the other saints who reposed within that church,—offered the most tranquil security to its people and those who took refuge in it, and afforded them all a perfectly safe asylum from hostile assaults. Nevertheless, at first the Picts rushed with impetuous haste to the river Tyne, on which the town stands, and would have destroyed it, as they had others; but just as they were about to cross this river, two of their number were killed by their own countrymen, and on this the others retired in fear. Moreover, two of the same tribe of Picts came by chance upon an oratory of St. Michael the archangel, situated on that, the northern bank of the river Tyne, and attached to the aforesaid church of Hexham; thereupon they broke open the door, and carried off what they found. But the vengeance of God overtook them; for, given up to the evil one, they were bereft of reason, and, as the madness drove them, tore night and day, in the sight of all, through forest and country, and both perished by a horrible death; the one first battering his own face with stones, and then having his legs cut off by some one, the other drowning himself in the Tyne. These events striking terror into some of the army, they did not venture to make any further attempt upon the possessions of the church of Hexham. Thereupon David, king of Scotland, and earl Henry his son, guaranteed to that monastery, its brethren, and all belonging to it, continued security from hostilities on the part of themselves and all their followers; and this they confirmed by their charters, which are preserved in that church, the sole condition being that they, on their part, should preserve the peace towards him and his. Thus that noble church, founded by St. Wilfrid, preserving its ancient and wonted lustre in this and other storms of battle and contention, became a secure place of refuge to numberless poor as well as rich, to whom it afforded the necessaries of life, and the preservation of their property.

Meanwhile, about the feast of the Purification of St. Mary [2d Feb.], Stephen, king of England, arrived with a great number of earls and barons, and a large force of horse and foot. On hearing of this the king of Scotland left Northumberland, and rapidly retreated with his army to his own territory. He marched to Wark, and afterwards lay in wait with his troops in some wilds near Roxburgh, with a design to ensnare the king of England, who he hoped would take up his quarters at Roxburgh. He directed the citizens to receive him favourably, and to make a show of good faith; but he also directed that when he with his army should steal up by night, and a number of soldiers whom he had placed in the town should make a sudden sally and join him with the townsmen, they all should unite in encompassing the king of England unawares on every side, and should cut him off with all his men. But the Lord, who knoweth the thoughts of man that they are but vain, brought to nought all these devices. For the king of England crossed the river Tweed, and did not proceed to Roxburgh, but devastated and burnt a great portion

of the territory of the king of Scotland ; and then, because many of
his knights declined to take arms and carry on the war, (for it was
now the beginning of Lent,)[1] and also because the king of Scotland
and his men dared not give battle, and moreover, his own army
was deficient in supplies, he therefore retired with his troops
to the south of England, But, on the Friday of the week following the celebration of Easter [15th April], the king of Scotland,
so frequently mentioned, with his execrable army, once more
returned to Northumberland, and with no less ferocity and cruelty
than he had previously exhibited, he devastated first the sea-coast
of the county, which on the former occasion had been left undis-
turbed, and all those other portions besides which anywhere had
escaped uninjured, and after that the greater part of the territory of
St. Cuthbert, on the eastern side, between Durham and the sea.
And both on this and the former occasion he in like manner
destroyed, together with the husbandmen, many farms of the
monks who served God and St. Cuthbert day and night.   But
St. Cuthbert at length took pity on his servants ; for, whilst his
adherents were perpetrating these enormities, the king with his
retinue took up his abode near Durham, and there a serious
mutiny having arisen on account of a certain woman, the life of the
king and his suite was placed in jeopardy by the Picts.   Whilst
under much apprehension from this danger, suddenly a false report
was spread that a large army was approaching from the south
of Britain ; so he with all his forces, leaving untouched their provisions already prepared, fled unpursued towards their own country,
and marching to Norham, which is in the territory of St. Cuthbert,
and laying siege to it, endeavoured to assault and reduce it by
various plans and devices.   And while he remained there occupied
in the siege, he despatched his nephew William, son of Duncan, on
an expedition into Yorkshire, with the Picts and a portion of his
army.   When they had arrived there, and had gained the victory,
on account of the sins of the people, they destroyed by fire and
sword the main part of the possessions of a splendid monastery
situated in Southerness, and in the district called Craven.   Then,
sparing no rank, no age, no sex, no condition, they first massacred, in
the most barbarous manner possible, children and kindred in the
sight of their relatives, masters in sight of their servants, and
servants in the sight of their masters, and husbands before the eyes
of their wives ; and then (horrible to relate) they carried off, like
so much booty, the noble matrons and chaste virgins, together
with other women.   These naked, fettered, herded together, by
whips and thongs they drove before them, goading them with their
spears and other weapons.   This took place in other wars, but in
this to a far greater extent.   Afterwards, when they were distributed
along with the other booty, a few from motives of pity restored
some of them to liberty, at the church of St. Mary in Carlisle ; but
the Picts and many others carried off those who fell to their share,
to their own country.   And finally, these brutal men, making no
account of adultery, incest, or such crimes, when tired of abusing

[1] Ash-Wednesday fell this year upon February 16.

these poor wretches like unto animals, made them their slaves, or sold them for cattle to other barbarians.

The king of Scots and his men received these tidings with great exultation, and applied themselves to the capture of the fortress before-named with still greater energy. The townsmen at first defended themselves with great vigour, but afterwards being few, and many of them wounded, (there being only nine knights,) despairing also of aid from their lord Geoffrey, bishop of Durham, and being besides inexperienced in such struggles, they in dismay surrendered to the king, while as yet the wall was in good condition, the tower very strong, and their provisions abundant. The soldiers, consequently, and those who were in the town, incurred great obloquy, because they had made a feeble resistance, and had too readily given up the castle; and not only were they censured, but their lord also, because he had not garrisoned his fortress according to his means, and as the necessities of the period required. The knights retired with their men to Durham. So the king, having captured the town, and taken the provisions which were there stored up in much abundance, intimated to the bishop that if he would desert Stephen, king of England, and swear fealty to his party, he would restore the castle to him, and make good the damage which it had sustained. This the bishop refused, and the king, therefore, caused the town to be dismantled.

While these events occurred there, about Rogation [1] time, the soldiers sallying from the town of Wark, seized under their walls king David's supplies, which had to pass close by them, together with the waggons and the attendants. The king, excessively enraged at this, hastened with his whole force to besiege them, and by batteries and all the means in his power he again proceeded to assail it. But by God's blessing all his endeavours fell fruitless. Many of his men were wounded and disabled, and some slain; likewise, in the conflicts which before this siege had been fought with the king's son Henry, some were killed, others wounded or taken prisoners, and ransom received for them. Blessed be God over all, who protecteth the righteous, but overthroweth the wicked! The king then, perceiving that his attempts upon the town were useless, caused the crops to be consumed on the ground, and then levying from his own country, and whencesoever else he could, a larger force than ever before, he united his troops into one body. Moreover Eustace Fitz-John, one of the barons of the king of England, who held a very strong fortress in Northumberland, called Alnwick, and had long secretly favoured the king of Scotland, now openly showing his treachery, threw off his allegiance to his lawful sovereign, the king of England, and with his whole strength gave his aid to the Scots against the realm of England. Leading with him no inconsiderable number of fighting men, he marched with the king of Scotland to ravage Yorkshire, and had made arrangements to give up to the king of Scotland and his party another strong castle of his called Malton, situated in that province on the river Derwent, not far from York, of which we shall

---

[1] Rogation Sunday fell upon May 8.

have to say more hereafter. King David then, consigning the siege of Wark to two of the thanes (that is to say, his barons), with their retainers, marched with most of his army to the town called Bamborough, where having taken an outwork of the castle, he killed nearly a hundred men. And then having destroyed the crops around that place, and around William Bertram's town of Mitford, and in many other parts of Northumberland, he crossed the river Tyne. Entering the territory of St. Cuthbert, he there waited for a portion of his army which had not yet joined him, and at his summons the Picts, and Cumbrians, and the men of Carlisle and the adjoining district, came to him without delay. The whole army being thus assembled, he regarded it with unbounded exultation; for it appeared to him immense and invincible, and in truth it was very large, consisting of more than twenty-six thousand men. His heart and the hearts of his men were lifted up, and putting their trust in themselves and their numbers, and having no fear of God, they spoke boastfully and proudly. They both designed and threatened to give to destruction not only Yorkshire, but the greatest part of England; for, with such a host, they did not imagine that any one would venture or be able to resist them. These transactions occurred within the octave of the Nativity of St. Mary [8—15th Sept.]; and the king then passing by Durham, destroyed the crops as far as the river Tees, and, according to his usual practice, caused the towns and churches which had previously escaped uninjured to be dismantled, plundered, and burnt. Crossing the Tees, he commenced a similar career of violence. But God's mercy, being moved by the tears of innumerable widows, orphans, and victims, no longer permitted such wickedness to remain unchastised. For whilst he and his men were engaged in this course of outrage, information of his crimes, his proceedings, and his designs was conveyed to the men of Yorkshire, both by common report and by sure intelligence; whereupon the barons of that province, to wit, archbishop Turstin (who, as will presently appear, greatly exerted himself in this emergency), William de Albemarle, Walter de Gant, Robert de Bruce, Roger de Mowbray, Walter Espec, Ilbert de Lacy, William de Percy, Richard de Courcy, William Fossard, Robert de Stuteville, and other powerful and sagacious men, assembled at York, and anxiously deliberated as to what course should be pursued at this crisis. Much irresolution was caused by distrust of each other, arising from suspicions of treachery, by the absence of a chief and leader of the war (for their sovereign, king Stephen, encompassed by equal difficulties in the south of England, was just then unable to join them), and by their dread of encountering, with an inadequate force, so great a host; so that it appeared as if they would actually have abandoned the defence of themselves and their country, had not their archbishop, Turstin, a man of great firmness and worth, animated them by his counsel and exhortations. For, being the shepherd of their souls, he would not, like a hireling on the approach of the wolf, seek safety in flight, but rather, pierced with the deepest emotions of pity at the dispersion and ruin of his flock, he applied all his

energy and labours to counteract these great evils. Wherefore, by the
authority of his divine commission, and the royal warrant with which
on that occasion he was provided, he boldly urged them, by their
loyalty and their honour, not to allow themselves through cowardice
to be prostrated at one blow by utter savages; but that rather they
all, with their dependants, should seek God's favour by true re-
pentance, and turning with all their heart to Him whose wrath
these many and heavy evils proved that they deserved, they should
then act with the confidence and courage demanded in so pressing
an emergency.   If they acted thus devotedly, trusting in God's
mercy, he assured them of victory; for that infamous people were
directing their hostile endeavours against God and holy church
rather than against them, and therefore were fighting in a cause un-
righteous, nay rather accursed.   But their cause was a just and most
holy one, inasmuch as they were encountering peril in defence of
holy church and of their country; and if so be it should please God
that this contest should not terminate without the loss of some of
them, yet, by those who were fighting with such an object, death was
not to be feared, but rather desired.   He promised them also, that
the priests of his diocese, bearing crosses, should march with them to
battle with their parishioners, and that he also, God willing, designed
to be present with his men in the engagement.

At this period of perplexity one of the nobles of that province,
Bernard de Baliol, sent to them by the king of England, arrived
with a number of knights; and, on the king's part and his own, he
greatly aroused their energy to the same effect.   Thus incited by
the charge of the king and their archbishop, coming unanimously
to one decision, they returned to their own abodes; and shortly
after again met at York, each fully equipped and armed for battle.
Having there made private confession, the archbishop enjoined on
them and the whole populace a three days' fast with almsgiving;
after which he solemnly absolved them, and gave them God's
blessing and his own.   And although he was himself so greatly
reduced by age and infirmity, that he had to be carried on a litter
where need was, yet, in order to animate their courage, he would
readily have accompanied them to the field of battle.   But they
compelled him to stay behind, begging that he would employ himself in interceding for them by prayers and alms, by vigils and fasts,
and other sacred observances; while they (as God would deign to
aid them, and as their position demanded) would cheerfully go
forth against the enemy, in defence of God's church, and of him
who was his minister.   So he consigned to them his cross, and the
standard of St. Peter, and his retainers; and they proceeded to the
town called Thirsk, from whence they despatched Robert de Bruce
and Bernard de Baliol to the king of Scotland, who was then, as
has been said, devastating the territory of St. Cuthbert.   They very
humbly and courteously besought him that he would at least desist
from his acts of ferocity; and faithfully promised him that if he
would accede to their request, they would obtain from the king of
England the earldom of Northumberland, which he claimed for his
son Henry.   But he, together with his followers, with a hardened

heart, spurned their solicitation, and disdainfully taunted them. They therefore returned to their associates, Robert abjuring the homage he had rendered him, and Bernard the fealty which he had sworn to him on one occasion when he had been taken prisoner by him.   All the nobles, therefore, of that province, and William Peverel and Geoffrey Halsalin from Nottinghamshire, and Robert de Ferrers from Derbyshire, and other eminent and sagacious men, made a compact amongst themselves, which they confirmed by oaths, that not one of them, in this difficulty, would desert another while he had the power to aid him; and thus all would either perish or conquer together.   At the same time the archbishop sent to them Ralph, surnamed Novellus, bishop of Orkney, with one of his archdeacons and other clergy, who, as his delegate, should impose penance and give absolution to the people who daily flocked to them from every quarter.   He also sent to them, as he had promised, the priests with their parishioners.   While thus waiting the approach of the Scots, the scouts whom they had sent forward to reconnoitre returned, bringing the information that the king with his army had already passed the river Tees, and was ravaging their province in his wonted manner: They therefore hastened to resist them; and passing the village of Alverton [North Allerton], they arrived early in the morning at a plain distant from it about two miles.   Some of them soon erected, in the centre of a frame which they brought, the mast of a ship, to which they gave the name of the Standard; whence those lines of Hugh Sotevagina,[1] archdeacon of York :—

> " Our gallant *stand* by all confest,
>   Be this the *Standard's* fight;
> Where death or victory the test,
>   That proved the warriors' might."

On the top of this pole they hung a silver pix containing the Host, and the banner of St. Peter the Apostle, and John of Beverley and Wilfrid of Ripon, confessors and bishops.   In doing this, their hope was that our Lord Jesus Christ, by the efficacy of his Body, might be their leader in the contest in which they were engaging in defence of his church and their country.   By this means they also provided for their men, that, in the event of their being cut off and separated from them, they might observe some certain and conspicuous rallying-point, by which they might rejoin their comrades, and where they would receive succour.

Scarcely, then, had they put themselves in battle array, when tidings were brought that the king of Scotland was close at hand with his whole force, ready and eager for the contest.   The greater part of the knights, then dismounting, became foot soldiers, a chosen body of whom, interspersed with archers, were arranged in the front rank.   The others, with the exception of those who were to dispose and rally the forces, mustered with the barons in the centre, near and around the standard, and were enclosed by the rest of the host, who closed in on all sides.   The troop of cavalry

---

[1] Some of the poems of this individual are preserved in the Cotton MS. Vitell. A. xii., in which he is styled chanter and archdeacon of the church of St. Peter's of York.

and the horses of the knights were stationed at a little distance, lest they should take fright at the shouting and uproar of the Scots. In like manner, on the enemy's side, the king and almost all his followers were on foot, their horses being kept at a distance. In front of the battle were the Picts; in the centre, the king with his knights and English;[1] the rest of the barbarian host poured roaring around them.

As they advanced in this order to battle, the standard with its banners became visible at no great distance; and at once the hearts of the king and his followers were overpowered by extreme terror and consternation; yet, persisting in their wickedness, they pressed on to accomplish their bad ends. On the octaves of the Assumption of St. Mary, being Monday, the eleventh of the kalends of September [22d Aug.], between the first and third hours, the struggle of this battle was begun and finished. For numberless Picts being slain immediately on the first attack, the rest, throwing down their arms, disgracefully fled. The plain was strewed with corpses; very many were taken prisoners; the king and all the others took to flight; and at length, of that immense army all were either slain, captured, or scattered as sheep without a shepherd. They fled like persons bereft of reason, in a marvellous manner, into the adjoining district of their adversaries, increasing their distance from their own country, instead of retreating towards it. But wherever they were discovered, they were put to death like sheep for the slaughter; and thus, by the righteous judgment of God, those who had cruelly massacred multitudes, and left them unburied, and giving them neither their country's nor a foreign rite of burial,—left a prey to the dogs, the birds, and the wild beasts,—were either dismembered and torn to pieces, or decayed and putrefied in the open air. The king also, who, in the haughtiness of his mind and the power of his army, seemed a little before to reach with his head even to the stars of heaven, and threatened ruin to the whole or greatest part of England, now dishonoured and meanly attended, barely escaped with his life, in the utmost ignominy and dismay. The power of Divine vengeance was also most plainly exhibited in this, that the army of the vanquished was incalculably greater than that of the conquerors. No estimate could be formed of the number of the slain; for, as many affirm, of that army which came out of Scotland alone, it was computed by the survivors that more than ten thousand were missing; and in various localities of the Deirans, Bernicians, Northumbrians, and Cumbrians, many more perished after the fight than fell in the battle.

The army of the English having, by God's help, with a small loss, thus easily obtained the victory, and taken possession of the spoil, which was found in great abundance, was very speedily disbanded; and all returning to their homes, they restored with joy and thanksgiving to the churches of the saints the banners which they had received. They had gone forth to this battle in their gayest array, and with costly splendour, as to a royal marriage. Some of the

---

[1] That is, those of Saxon or Norman origin, as distinguished from the Celtic inhabitants of Scotland.

barons, with a portion of the army, marched to Eustace's town, called Malton, mentioned above; and having destroyed the suburb, they laid siege to it, because, during the fight, the soldiers had sallied from it by orders of their lord, and set fire to many villages. A truce of eight days was arranged, after which the siege continued. The ground on which the above battle was fought was alone the possession of St. Cuthbert, the whole surrounding district being owned by others; and this occurred not by design of the combatants, but by the dispensation of Providence; for it may clearly be observed that Divine justice would not long allow to go unpunished the iniquity that had been perpetrated in the territory of his holy and beloved confessor and bishop, but would speedily visit it with wonted vengeance.

The king of England received the news of this event with extreme joy; and, being informed that they had greatly distinguished themselves in this affair, he created William de Albemarle earl in Yorkshire, and Robert de Ferrers earl in Derbyshire. And it is to be remarked that, about this time, fortune in a like manner befriended himself and his supporters, both in the south of England and in Normandy, in their encounters with their opponents. The king of Scotland added fresh force to the siege of Wark, upon being rejoined by his son Henry, and reassembling his men, who had fled from the fight separately, rather like bitter foes than comrades; for when these Angles, Scots, Picts, and other barbarians, experience a disaster, those who have the power either murder, wound, or at the least despoil the others, and then, by the righteous judgment of God, they were cut off by their allies as well as their foes. The king, upon hearing these facts, imposed upon his subjects heavy penalties and fines, and drew from them an immense sum of money; at the same time, he bound them more strongly than ever before, by oaths and pledges, never more to abandon him in war. He then endeavoured by engines, new constructions, and various devices, to gain possession of the town of Wark. The townsmen, however, destroyed his engines, killed in various ways several of the king's men, and wounded many, with a loss of only one of their own soldiers, who was cut off and slain by a multitude of the Scots who had sallied from the castle, and he, rashly confident in his own valour, was staying to demolish one of the engines. The king at length, seeing all his endeavours ineffectual, and damaging to himself and his troops, removed his engines relinquished the assault, and enforced a strict blockade of the town, much against the inclination of his followers; for in consequence of the great losses, difficulties, and destitution which they had there endured, they were completely worn out by the protracted siege.

At this time certain lawless persons, whose sole study and delight was to plan and perpetrate crimes, banded themselves together in a detestable alliance, the more effectually to carry out their designs of mischief. The chiefs and leaders of this abominable fraternity were Edgar, the illegitimate son of earl Cospatrick, and Robert and Uctred, sons of Meldred. Urged, therefore, by rapacity, encouraged by impunity, and frenzied by passion, they overran

Northumberland like-wolves, seeking whom they might devour;
and crossing the river Tyne, they came upon the territory of St.
Cuthbert, but lighting upon nothing there which it was within
their power or their daring to seize, they returned empty-handed.
They then carried off all the booty they could obtain in a village of
the parish of Hexham, called Herintun [Errington]. Two nights
after these same robbers attacked another village called Digentun
[Denton]. This village was the property of the canons of the church
aforesaid, and was distant eight miles east of Hexham. Having slain
three of the canons' servants, and heaped many insults on their
prior, who had happened to arrive unexpectedly that night, they
marched off with their spoil. This mischance befel these canons
contrary to their expectation, inasmuch as the king of Scotland
had promised, as well for himself as for all his followers, (as was
before said,) the most absolute security to them, their vassals, their
effects, their parish, and expressly this very village.

About this period Alberic, bishop of Ostia, arrived in these
parts, having been sent by pope Innocent to fulfil the office of
legate in England and Scotland. By birth he was a Frenchman,
by profession a monk of the Clugniac order, eminent for learning,
sacred and secular, of much experience in ecclesiastical affairs, of
remarkable eloquence and sound judgment; and, what is far beyond
all this, he gave proof in demeanour and appearance, and in fact in
his whole conversation and conduct, of great goodness and piety. Entering Clugny on his first profession, he, by his discretion and piety,
attained the office of sub-prior, where, in consequence, the whole
charge of the ritual observance came under his supervision. Afterwards, in France, he for some time filled the office of prior in the
religious house known as St. Martin des Champs; but inasmuch
as he was of great service, and in high esteem amongst his brethren, he was some years after recalled to occupy the position of
sub-prior at home. From this he was chosen to preside as abbot
over the monastery of Vezeley,[1] and thence, by canonical election,
he was elevated to the bishopric of the church of Ostia. To the
bishops of this church pertained, by a dignity of long standing, the
privilege of consecrating the pope himself. Coming (as we have
said) to England, he afforded to all his faithful sons much satisfaction as to the condition of the holy mother church of Rome; for
the sovereign pontiff above named sent by him his epistle to all the
children of the Catholic church. In it he related how the vessel
of St. Peter had toiled on heavily, having been long and violently
agitated by opposing billows, and thrown, shaken and shattered, on
the rocks of schismatics, and was well-nigh past hope of recovery,
since, unhappily, for eight years it had been exposed to havoc and
pollution, inexpressible and accursed, which had been inflicted
on it by that first-born of Satan, Petrus Leo,[2] and his supporters.
But this there was no need to dwell upon, for it had been known
and lamented by almost the whole world. But the infinite mercy

---

[1] A monastery in the diocese of Autun. See concerning it and this individual,
Mabill. Annal. ord. S. Bened. A.D. 1138, § 16.
[2] Anaclet II., reckoned among the antipopes. See Baron. Annal. A.D. 1130, § 2.

of Christ, though it seemed to slumber, and, for our sins, to pay no regard, nevertheless, moved at length and aroused by the earnest prayers and tears of his faithful people, stilled by the mighty word of his power the raging of the sea, the violence of the winds, and the fury of the tempest, changing the storm into a favouring breeze. He brought the church to rest in the haven of peace and the joy of security. Moreover, He turned the arrogance and glorying of all her enemies to prostration and ignominy, and brought the necks of all who opposed her under the yoke of her power. We may therefore justly exclaim with the Psalmist, " O Lord our Governor, how excellent is thy name in all the world, Thou that hast set thy glory above the heavens." [Ps. viii. 1.]

Besides the epistle which thus spoke of the recovery of peace and unity to the holy Roman church, and the restoration of the apostolic power and dignity, Alberic brought also letters warranting his mission, addressed by the pope aforesaid to the kings of England and Scotland, to Thurstin, archbishop of York, (the metropolitan see of Canterbury being at that time vacant,) and to the bishops, abbots, and prelates of holy church in both kingdoms ; he was therefore received by all with respect. He also brought with him from the continent the abbot[1] of the monastery of Molesme, with several monks ; and immediately on his arrival in England he summoned to his side one other, named Richard, abbot of the monastery called Fountains, a very religious man of great influence : these truly wise and virtuous men were the constant companions and witnesses of his life and course of action. In order that he might avail himself of their advice and assistance in the transaction of affairs, and that by their testimony the uprightness of his conduct might be fully evidenced, he made the circuit of nearly the whole of England, visiting the cathedral churches and the monasteries of both clerics and monks, at each of which he was received with due reverence. He at length reached Durham, where at this time William Cumin, chancellor of David, king of Scotland, was kept in confinement, having been taken prisoner in his flight from the battle above mentioned. He delivered him at once from his imprisonment, and restored him in freedom to his sovereign. Then, accompanied by two bishops, Robert of Hereford and Athelwulf of Carlisle, three abbots, and several clergy, he came over the moors to the monastery of Hexham, at which place he was entertained by the brethren with all fitting honour ; and with much consideration, he cheered them under the injury which they had recently sustained by the loss of their men and the pillaging of their territory, as we have just narrated. Passing thence through Northumberland and Cumberland, he arrived at Carlisle four days before the feast of St. Michael [29th Sept.], and there met the king of Scotland, with the bishops, abbots, priors, and barons of his country. They, differing widely from the Cisalpine—and indeed from almost the whole church—appear to have inclined in

---

[1] Everard, abbot of the Benedictine monastery of Molesme, in the diocese of Langres.

a great degree to the schism of Peter Leo of execrable memory; but now, through the influence of Divine grace, they one and all received with great veneration the missive of pope Innocent and his legate. For three days, then, he was busily employed with them on the affairs of his mission. He was informed that John, bishop of Glasgow, committing to no one the cure of souls which he held, had clandestinely, without leave, resigned his bishopric, and, for no apparent reason, had become a monk at Tiron; whereupon he determined in his case that a king's messenger, with letters from himself and the king, should be sent for him, and in the event of his refusal to return home, that sentence should be pronounced against him; and this was done accordingly. He also negotiated with the king concerning the renewal of a peace between him and the king of England, and on this behalf entreated him to take pity on holy church, and on himself and his people, on whom he had brought so many and great evils; but he with difficulty obtained a suspension of hostilities, to the extent that, excepting the investment of Wark, he would send no force, and make no aggression upon the territory of the king of England before the feast of St. Martin [11th Nov.]. He also obtained this from the Picts, that before the same period they would bring to Carlisle all the girls and women whom they held captive, and there restore them to liberty. They also, and all the others, promised him most faithfully that they would not again in any way violate churches, and that they would spare children and females, and persons enfeebled by age and infirmity, and, in short, would slay none but those engaged in actual conflict. Moreover, the king, unsolicited, discoursed with the prior of Hexham, who had come with the legate, concerning the loss sustained by himself and his brethren, which he much lamented, and for which he promised full indemnification, and also that he would compel his people to make amends for the injury done to them and their church, and for the slaughter of their men. And this he in a great measure fulfilled; for nearly all their property, and that of their vassals, was restored.

These affairs being thus arranged, the legate taking his departure on the feast of St. Michael [29th Sept.], returned by way of Hexham and Durham to the south of England, and related to Stephen, king of England, what he had accomplished with David, king of Scotland, and his people. The king of Scotland, a few days after, learnt from some who had come out of Wark, that those in the town were reduced to great extremity by famine; and, in consequence, he enforced a still more strict blockade. This indeed was the case, for the garrison, from want of provisions, had killed and salted their horses, and had already consumed the greater part of them, but were, nevertheless, unwilling to surrender the town, and indeed designed, when food altogether failed them, to sally armed from the fortress, charge through the enemy, and defend themselves to the last, unless in the meanwhile God should provide for them some other resource. About the feast of St. Martin [11th Nov.], William, abbot of Rievaux, came into that province, and, on the part of Walter Espec, to whom, as before said, the town belonged,

charged them to yield it to the king of Scotland, for he was well
aware how wofully they were reduced by famine. The king thereupon, by the mediation of the abbot, gave them twenty-five horses,
and allowed them to march out with their arms; and being put in
possession of the town, he speedily caused it to be dismantled.
The above-named legate, on his return, as before mentioned, from
his visitation of the sees and monasteries to the court of the king
of England, met there another legate, who had just arrived from
the sovereign pope Innocent. They consequently issued a summons to Thurstin, archbishop of York, and all the bishops, abbots,
and priors of canons throughout England, to assemble at a general
council in the city of London, on the feast of St. Nicholas [6th
Dec.]. They met at the appointed time and place with Stephen,
king of England, and both legates entered with them upon the
discussion of the affairs of the church; Alberic, however, took
precedence. The council was to the following effect:—

"In the year of our Lord 1138, the ninth year of the ponti-
ficate of the sovereign pope Innocent the second, the third year of
the reign of the most pious and illustrious Stephen, king of the
English, nephew of the great king Henry, the synod of London
was held in the church of St. Peter, the chief of the apostles, at
Westminster, in the month of December, on the thirteenth day of
the month, at which, after the discussion of many questions, these
canons, seventeen in number, were issued and unanimously confirmed. Alberic, bishop of Ostia, and legate in England and
Scotland of the aforesaid pope Innocent, presided over this synod,
where there were assembled eighteen bishops of various provinces,
about thirty abbots, and a countless multitude of clergy and laity.
The see of Canterbury was at that time vacant, and Thurstin,
archbishop of York, was out of health, but he sent thither William,
dean of the church of St. Peter at York, with some of his clergy.
The following are the canons:—

"'Following the canonical institutes of the holy fathers, we, by
apostolic authority, prohibit the exaction of any fee whatever for
chrisms, for oil, for baptism, for absolution, for the visitation of the
sick, for the betrothal of women, for unction, for the communion
of Christ's Body, or for burial. Whoever shall dare to do so, let
him be excommunicate.

"'We enact, also, that the Body of Christ be not received beyond
eight days, and be not carried to the sick except by the priest or
deacons, or, in extreme necessity, by some other, and this with the
greatest reverence.

"'Likewise we enact, by apostolic authority, that at the consecration of bishops, and the benediction of abbots, neither a hood, nor
ecclesiastical vestment, nor anything be demanded from the bishop
or his ministers; and also, in the consecration of churches, no demand shall be made for tapestry, towel, or basin, or anything beyond
the fee allowed by the sacred canons.

"'When any bishop shall procure the consecration of a church in
his diocese by another bishop, we, by apostolic authority, prohibit
any demand being made beyond that bishop's fee.

"'No one shall receive from lay hands a church, or any ecclesiastical benefice whatever. When any one receives investiture from the bishop, we direct that he shall take oath upon the Gospels that he has not on this account given or promised anything to any one by himself or another; and where this has been done, the presentation shall be void, and both giver and acceptor shall be subject to canonical judgment.

"'We further enact, that no one shall claim by inheritance any church or other ecclesiastical benefice held by his father; and no one shall appoint a successor to himself in any ecclesiastical benefice; and where this is done we decree it to be void, saying, with the Psalmist, "O my God, make them like unto a wheel who have said, Let us take to ourselves the houses of God in possession," [Ps. lxxxiii. 13.]

"'Clergy ordained by other than their own bishops, without letters dimissory, we suspend from the functions of the orders which they have received, and their plenary restitution shall rest with the Roman pontiff alone, unless they assume the religious habit.

"'Walking in the steps of the holy fathers, we deprive of ecclesiastical functions and benefices all priests, deacons, and subdeacons, married or living in concubinage, and, by apostolic authority, we forbid all persons from hearing a mass celebrated by such.

"'We decree the removal from every ecclesiastical function and benefice of those clergy who practise usury, or follow filthy lucre, or engage in secular business.

"'If any one shall kill, imprison, or assault any cleric, monk, nun, or any ecclesiastical person whatever, unless at the third summons he make satisfaction, he shall be excommunicate. Nor shall any one except the Roman pontiff give him absolution, unless at the point of death; and if he die impenitent, his body shall not receive sepulture.

"'Whosoever shall seize by violence the property of churches, whether moveable or fixed, we pronounce him excommunicate, unless after canonical citation he make amends.

"'We, by apostolic authority, prohibit any one from founding on his estate a church or oratory without licence from the bishop.

"'To these we subjoin the judgment of pope Nicholas, who says, "Inasmuch as the soldiers of Christ differ from the soldiers of the world, it is not meet that the soldier of the church should engage in secular warfare, of which the shedding of blood must be the result. In short, as it is disgraceful that a laic perform mass, or administer the sacrament of the Body and Blood of Christ, so it is absurd and improper for a cleric to bear arms or engage in war; as the apostle Paul says, 'No man that warreth for God entangleth himself,' &c. (2 Tim. ii. 4.)"

"'We likewise approve the judgment of pope Innocent, communicated to Victricus, archbishop of Rouen, that monks who after residing in monasteries are advanced to the priesthood, should not in any degree deviate from their former rule; in the clerical rank they ought to live as when they resided in their monasteries, and not to abandon in a higher position the order which they have long observed.

"'By apostolic authority, we forbid nuns to use skins of vair or gris, sable, marten, ermine, or beaver, to wear gold rings, or to practise curling or braiding of the hair: whosoever shall be detected in the violation of this law shall be excommunicated.

"' By apostolic authority, we decree due tithes of all first-fruits to be paid : any one who shall refuse payment of these tithes shall incur sentence of excommunication.

"' We further enact, that schoolmasters who shall let for hire the teaching of their schools to others, shall be liable to ecclesiastical censure.' "

The election of an archbishop to the see of Canterbury (which, as has been said, was then vacant) was agitated at this council, and this matter was brought to a conclusion after the following Epiphany, when the abbot of the monastery of Bec, Theobald by name, was consecrated[1] by the aforesaid Alberic, archbishop of that church. At the same council the abbot of Croyland was deposed, and another substituted in his room, namely, Godfrey, prior of the church of St. Alban the Martyr ; and Adam was elected abbot of the abbey near Hastings, called Battle: upon both of these the aforesaid Alberic bestowed the benediction. He also invited all the bishops and many of the abbots of England to a general council, which the sovereign pope Innocent was about to hold at Rome in the middle of Lent. During the course of these proceedings, he was engaged most discreetly and earnestly in treating with several persons, and especially with the queen of England, respecting the renewal of peace between the two kings. Finding that the queen's mind was much set upon the accomplishment of this object, with her mediation, and backed by her feminine shrewdness and address, he frequently appealed to the king himself regarding this matter. They found him at first stern, and apparently opposed to a reconciliation ; for many of his barons who had suffered severe losses from their variance, eagerly urged him on no account to make peace with the king of Scotland, but boldly to avenge himself upon him ; but notwithstanding all this, the zeal of a woman's heart, ignoring defeat, persisted night and day in every species of importunity, till it succeeded in bending the king's mind to its purpose. For she was warmly attached to her uncle David, king of Scotland, and his son Henry, her cousin, and on that account took the greatest pains to reconcile them to her husband. The legate, seeing the affair progressing in this way, derived fresh confidence in his intercourse with the king, from the better hope which had sprung up, and gave his attention to his other concerns.

A.D. 1139. The legate, so frequently mentioned, having completed his business in England, repaired to the coasts with his associates soon after the octave of the Epiphany [Jan. 13], and crossed the sea on his return ; for he hastened to attend at the appointed time the council of the sovereign pope before mentioned. To represent the bishops and abbots of England, there went to the same council these five bishops, Theobald, archbishop of Canterbury, Ernulf, bishop of Rochester, Simon of Worcester, Roger

[1] He was consecrated 8th January, 1139. Le Neve, i. 8.

of Coventry, and Robert of Exeter, and with them four abbots; for king Stephen would not send any more on account of the troubles of his kingdom, which were then very great. Moreover Thurstin, of happy memory, archbishop of York, sent thither Richard, abbot of Fountains, a highly excellent man, of whom we have spoken before, both on account of the council and of some other private business which he had commissioned him to transact; for it was generally asserted that he designed to relinquish his see, and to appoint in his stead, as archbishop of York, his own brother Audoenus, bishop of Evreux. But while this was in preparation, his envoy died at Rome, leaving the matter unaccomplished, and also his brother, who before his death had assumed the religious habit of the monks at Merton, departed[1] this life at that place. The archbishop of Canterbury, with his pall, the aforesaid bishops and abbots, when the council was over, and their business completed, returned safe and sound. Soon after the aforesaid legate had left England, peace was concluded between the two kings, by means of envoys, on these terms: Stephen, king of England, granted to Henry, son of David, king of Scotland, the earldom of Northumberland, except two towns, Newcastle and Bamburgh, with all the lands which he held before. But for these towns he was bound to give him towns of the same value in the south of England. He directed also that the barons who held of the earldom, as many as chose, might make acknowledgment for their lands to earl Henry, and do homage to him, saving the fealty which they had vowed to himself; and this the most of them did. The king of Scotland and his son Henry, with all their dependants, were bound thenceforward to remain for life amicable and faithful to Stephen, king of England. And to render their fidelity more secure, they were pledged to give him as hostages five earls of Scotland, the son of earl Cospatrick, the son of Hugh de Morville, the son of earl Fergus, the son of Mel . . ., and the son of Mac . . . . They were bound also to observe unalterably the laws, customs, and statutes which his uncle king Henry had established in the county of Northumberland. This agreement was signed at Durham on the fifth of the ides of April [April 9], by Henry, son of the king of Scotland, and their barons, in the presence of Matilda, queen of England, and many earls and barons of the south of England. This also was specially defined, that earl Henry could claim no right either over the territory of St. Cuthbert, or over that of St. Andrew in Hexham-shire, inasmuch as it appertained to the archbishop of York. Going with the queen to the court of king Stephen, he found him at Nottingham. What had been done at Durham being confirmed by him, he remained during the summer in southern England, frequenting the king's court, and incurring great expense in his service. In this year died Walter de Gant, who had assumed the monkish habit at Bardney; and Robert de Ferrers, who was earl of Derbyshire.

THE END OF THE BATTLE OF THE STANDARD.

[1] See Gallia Christ. xi. 575.

JORDAN FANTOSME'S CHRONICLE

OF THE

WAR BETWEEN THE ENGLISH AND THE SCOTS IN 1173 AND 1174.

HEAR a true story (may God bless you !)
Of the best sovereign who was ever in life.
A fancy has taken me to make verses, it is right that I should tell
     you them :
I hold him wise who corrects himself by others.
Gentle king of England, of the most bold courage,
At the coronation of your son do you not remember
That the homage from the hands of the king of Albany
You caused to be presented to him without having faith forsworn ?
Then you said to both : " May God curse those
10 Who would remove from you love or friendship !
Against all the people of the world, in strength and aid,
With my son remain, holding safe my lordship."
Afterwards between you and your son a deadly hatred sprung up.
Whence many a gentle knight has since lost his life,
Many a man has been unhorsed, many a saddle emptied,
Many a good buckler pierced, many a hauberk broken.
After this coronation and after this investiture
You filched from your son something of his lordship,
You took away from him his will ; he could not get possession:
20 Here grew war without love, the Lord God confound it !
    A king of land without honour does not know well what to do :
The young sovereign did not know it, the gentle [and] good ;
When he could not accomplish his will on account of his father,
He thought in his mind that he would oppose him :
He went away secretly, passed a ford of Loire,
Till he came to Saint-Denis he would neither eat nor drink,
Told the king of France all his business.
They sent for him of Flanders,[1] Philip the warrior,
And Matthew[2] of Boulogne, that he should come with his brother.
30 Great was this meeting, you never saw greater.
    King Lewis[3] of France was at Saint-Denis,
Wrongly was the war made against king Henry,[4]

---

[1] Philip of Flanders succeeded his father in 1168, and died at the siege of
Acre in 1191. See Art de vérif. les Dates, iii. 11.
[2] This Matthew became earl of Boulogne by his marriage with Mary, the
daughter of king Stephen, and died 25th July, 1173.
[3] Louis VII., consecrated king of France Oct. 25, 1131.
[4] This line is wanting in the Lincoln MS.

And held a great council of all his good friends;
About the old king of England was he so thoughtful
(That) nearly by sorrow went out of his mind gentle king Lewis,
When the count of Flanders had raised his face,
And said to the king of France: " Be not so thoughtful.
You have great baronage, valiant and powerful,
To make great damage upon your enemies.
40 In all your land it would be wrong that any vassal should remain,
Who could bear arms, or might not be too old,
Not to make you oath on the body of Saint-Denis
That the war was wrongly made against king Henry."
        Count Thibault [1] of France arose from his seat,
And said to the emperor where was his great baronage:
" Gentle king of Saint-Denis, rage seizes my body.
I am your liege-man by fealty and by homage,
I am quite ready to make war and to find a host;
I will serve you forty days in the first rank,
50 And I will do to king Henry, I think, such damage
That it will not be repaired in all his life;
He will not escape it anywhere in plain or wood,
If he give not back his heritage to his son the young king,
The kingdom of England, if he will act wisely.
You will leave him Normandy, if he appeases your wrath.
If there is anything mistaken and if I have said any too much,
Or anybody would prove it against me in his language,
Behold me here in your court ready to offer my gage.
This person is perjured to you, and seeks your shame."
60   Already are of one accord the king and his barons,
And send messengers through many regions;
King Henry they defy for those reasons,
Put the fair lands to great destruction.
In the month of April at Easter was the host of France summoned,
And they ride into the marches, they display their banners.
King Henry rides against them with spurs,
And had in his company ten thousand Brabençons
And many a gentle knight, Angevin and Gascon,
Who will cause to those of France ire and contention.
70   Very great was the host of France which Lewis brings.
To destroy the father the son takes very great pains,
When he has conquered and taken him in war he will lead him to
        Saint-Denis; [2]
But the king his father had promised him something else,
That he shall see many a flag and many a horse of price,
Many a shield lined white and red and grey,
And many a joust made against his enemies,
Before he should be in battle a recreant and conquered.
        The lord of England has in his heart a weight
Since his son makes war against him, whom he bred from infancy,

[1] Thibault V. count of Blois and Champagne, died in 1191, at the siege of
Acres. See L'Art de vérif. les Dates, ii. 618.
[2] This line occurs only in the Lincoln MS.

80 [And sees that those of Flanders have led him astray :
    They promised him the land of the English for certain ;][1]
    He would rather have died than lived that he (his son) should have
        the power,
    As long as he could strike with sword or lance.
    He drew up his baronage with brave countenance ;
    Goes against Lewis, the rich king of France,
    Against the count Philip, of whom you hear talk,
    And lord Matthew his brother, a knight of valour.
    God helped much the father the day, when he advanced,
    And showed a fair sign about his war ;
90 For the helpers of his son, in whom his hope most was,
    Were this day routed without any delay.
    It was Matthew the warrior, on whom came the lance ;
    King Henry shall have no more fear of him.
       The count of Boulogne has received a mortal wound,
    Down to his spurs of gold the red blood runs :
    He shall never recover, much though he try.
    The more his brother grieves, and the more he is dismayed himself ;
    And swears his oath, the precious wound,
    Never with king Henry he will be appeased.
100   Now rides Lewis, so does the young king,
    And Philip is put in great disarray.
    The count Thibault of France shows great pride.
    Soon king Henry shall know where to move himself :
    The French raise war against him, the Flemings and the Capei,[2]
    The earl of Leicester,[3] and there are also all his three sons.
    He of Tancarville[4] in truth does not love him ;
    One hundred knights at arms he brings in his retinue,
    Who all threaten to put him in such a disarray
    They will not leave him of land the worth of a palfrey.
110   Lords, by my troth, much marvel is there
    Why his vassals desire so to deal with him,
    [He who was] the most honourable and conquering
    That was in any land since the time of Moses,
    Except only king Charles, whose power was great
    Through the twelve companions Oliver and Roland.
       One has never heard in fable or in story
    Of one single king of his valour and great power.
    Although they all come threatening him, he swears by his head
    He will not cease to hawk by the river side or to hunt his beast.
120   Now rides the count Philip with his great host,
    And wastes Normandy by wood and plain.
    You would never have heard king Henry once complain of it,
    Nor ever seek occasion to stop the war.
    Much had the young king done, who bathes himself so well ;
    Still he has in his command the barons of Britany.

[1] These two lines are wanting in the Lincoln MS.
[2] The people of a place of Vermandois, which then belonged to the count of Flanders.   [3] Dugd. Baron. i. 87.
[4] William, the son of Rabel de Tancarville.

80

When the father heard it, he was sorry and angry,
And swears his oath that wrongly it was ever thought,
And said to his knights : " Lords, now hear me.
Never in my life was I so sorry.
130 Rage seizes my body, I am nearly mad.
The barons of Britany have already opposed me ;
To those who hate me to death they have abandoned themselves,
To king Lewis of France and to my eldest son,
Who come disinheriting me of what I possess.
He would rob me of my land and fiefs and heritages.
I am not so old, people know that enough,
That I should lose land on account of my great age.
With the still moon watch to-night,
In order that neither the Flemings nor the natives of the land be
        in ambush.
140 The barons of Britany, you know it well enough,
As far as Finistere, are in my power ;
But Raoul of Fougeres [1] has against me rebelled,
The earl Hugh [2] of Chester is bound to him :
I will not fail to see them for the cost of fine and pure gold,
If I could find them in their fortresses ;
And since our enemies are so confident,
Then it is well to invade them with a great hatred.
Craft is better than war against outlaws,
Than bad assault, if they are discouraged."
150 His baronage replies : " You are full of goodness.
All your enemies are entered into a bad year.
Yours is the land, so defend it ;
Wrongly wars against you your son."
    Now behold these knights gone down from the palace ;
And go to seize their arms quickly and forthwith,
Put on their hauberks and breastplates, lace their ornamented helms,
Take by the handles the Vianese shields.
Then you might hear the old king Henry call God to witness :
" Wrongly will the traitors have met me in the stubble-fields.'
160 From the town are issued knights in array,
Less than sixty [3] thousand and more than sixty-three ;
There is none of them who does not think himself as good as a
        Welsh king.
    Now rides king Henry with all his host,
Towards Dol in Britany he holds his way.
And said to William [4] of Humet, when he was in the expedition :
" Let us not talk of delay : behold their country.
    Those of the castle have already seen William and his banner,
And see that the Brabançons come all in the rear.
See the Norman host who will make us retreat.
170 Normans are good conquerors, there is nobody like them :
Everywhere we find it in story that Normans are victors.

[1] He succeeded his father in 1154, and died in 1196. L'Art, ii. 897.
[2] Dugd. Baron. i. 40.   [3] In the Lincoln MS. " thirty thousand."
[4] Dugd. Baron. i. 631.

Think of it, Sir Raoul, for the company is fierce.
The young king who wars against his father has betrayed us,
When he left the ways to be on the river.
I see no means how we can defend [ourselves];
They will receive neither silver nor gold, prayer will nought avail us."
   Raoul answers to this: " Folly has no business here,
Nor jest, nor joking, nor any levity;
But whoso knows good counsel, let him come forward and say it.
180 We have no fear to lose either life or limb.
The old king conducts himself with very great folly,
When he of Britany demands the seigniory.[1]
Threatens us for his possessions and his lands
But he shall not go as his pride guides him.
Such a counsel now let us take, without strife of anger,
That we be not to-day dishonoured, nor the land misgoverned.
This castle is not strong: let us not trust to it;
Let us go out against [them], so we will assail them."
   Then they charged each other in the middle of the plain,
190 Lord William of Humet and those of his company.
There is no knight of value who does not break there his lance.
Whoever would joust against a companion, soon found there his
   match.
By force were driven together the barons of Britany
Into their very fortresses; there is none who does not then com-
   plain of it.
By force was in his castle lord Raoul of Fougeres,
Hugh the earl of Chester proclaims himself a miserable sinner;
Neither mangonel nor stonebow was able to serve them.
The war which they have made shall be sold them dear,
For now goes a messenger to king Henry the father,
200 To Rouen in Normandy on a black horse used to rivers;
And told him what had happened to his fierce people,
To the earl of Chester, to Raoul of Fougeres.
Then he praises God the glorious and the glorious saint Peter:
" Discomfited are my enemies: alas that I was not there!"
   He gets ready his baronage, in which he trusts much;
Towards Dol in Britany he has taken his way;
But when he was come there with his knights,
Joyous he boasts of the fact to his followers.
Those who were in the castle did not rejoice at all,
210 They much fear his coming and dread his power;
They had not victuals enough to sustain their life,
They have surrendered themselves to king Henry, he holds them
   in his power.
   " Lords," quoth king Henry, " now counsel me:
My son is in the wrong towards me, it is meet that you know it;
For rent perforce he will have from my estates:
Reason, I think, there is none why it should be paid to him.
From a man of my power it is not to be thus extracted:
And that which is by force taken or gained

    [1] This line does not occur in the Durham MS.

Is nor right nor reasonable, so it is often judged.
220 To guard my franchise I am enough ill-treated,
And by those of Flanders often annoyed;
So we do not want more to be damaged.
You all together, lords, I pray that you aid me;
In pitched battle your strength essay,
With all your might for me strive:
Never you loved me, if at need you fail me.
Earl Hugh of Chester along with you take.
On Raoul of Fougeres I will execute my will;
I will leave him quite free within his estates,
230 By this condition that he be my liege.
If afterwards against me he rebels by any iniquity,
He shall hold in Britany neither estates nor heritages.
Arm, lords, your bodies; ride quickly:
My son is quite ready for the battle.
The rent he demands, let us pay it with our swords
And with keen brands and pointed darts."
For this news many are joyous and glad:
They are the knights the valiant and polite;
And the earl of Chester is grieved and wroth,
240 Nor hopes in his life to be disimprisoned.
Frightened are the French at the fierce tidings
The heart of the bravest trembles and staggers;
But he comforts them who leads them on.
Ire he has in his heart, his blood boils.
For counsel he goes to his most loyal men,
In romance he dictates a letter, with a ring seals it;
The messengers of the young king before him he calls:
It was king Lewis who gave the message.
Depart the messengers who bear the letters,
250 They pass the salt sea, the kingdoms traverse;
The forests, the plains, the dangerous fords they pass,
They come to Scotland and the king they find,
On the part of the young king Henry the writings present.
Now shall you hear the words which there were written:
" To the king of Scotland, William,[1] the best,
To whom our lineage was formerly ancestor.
The king Henry the young sends you by love,
You must remember me who am your lord.
It seems to me very marvellous, and I have fear in the heart,
260 Of so rich a king, of a man of thy valour,
Who has such strength of people and such vigour in himself,
That you will not help me in war, if you like, at first,
To war against my father, thou and thy counts.
I will give thee the land which thy ancestors had,
Thou never hadst from a king so great an estate in land,
The land beyond Tyne, under the heavens I do not know a better,
You shall have the lordship in castle and in tower;
We will give you Carlisle, that you may be stronger,

---

[1] William the Lion, who succeeded to the throne 24th Dec. 1165.

All Westmoreland without any contradiction,
270 That you help me with strength and readiness.
Drive away those who hold these lands."
     Now has the king of Scotland in his heart great sorrow
When he hears the command of the young king,
That he owes to him his homage against all people ;
On the other hand he sends him greeting as to a relation,
That he will give him his land which belongs to his estate,
Which all the kings of Scotland held in their life-time ;
And to the old king his father he owes likewise .
Homage and service, allegiance true.
280 It is not right that for promise he should act so boldly
That he should knowingly destroy the land of the old king,
Before he has claimed his inheritance.
If he means to contradict him, then let him do his pleasure,
Let him render his homage without pretext ;
And when he has rendered it to him, and if he takes it well,
Let him in any court deny the covenant ;
For the will of the prince is held as judgment.
Then held king William his plenary parliament ;
From the sages of his land he wished to have counsel,
290 If he should to the young king keep his oath.
There is none to contradict him or to forbid him.
     The king goes to consult with his baronage,
Tells them the news which they heard of the king :
The young one of England, who wars against his father,
Asks him for the land ; but he still refuses it.
" I will tell by messengers the father, in Normandy,
That he must give me back a part of my inheritance :
That is Northumberland, which he holds in his power ;
And if he will not do so and refuses it quite,
300 I owe him in future neither fealty nor friendship."
     Answers earl Duncan,[1] and says as a baron :
" The old king is reasonable, so let him have his right ;
Do not seek any opportunity of committing an outrage.
If he likes, you must serve him as his liege-man :
Let him restore you your rights without any subterfuge,
Then you will come to succour him with all speed.
Fair word exhibited by reason is better
Than threatening in asking for any gift ;
And whoever does otherwise, seeks destruction,
310 His own death and his damage and his confusion.'
     Earl Duncan has spoken very wisely ;
There is nobody who contradicts him, to my knowledge.
Then said the king himself, the barons and the people :
" This counsel is loyal, and it pleases me.
Let us send our messengers with this mandate,
And let them do their duty like valiant chevaliers."
     The messengers go, their horses they spur,
They slacken their reins on the great paved roads.

     [1] Duncan II. earl of Fife.

The horses are very good, which spring beneath them.
320 They come to Normandy, they do not stay long;
Find the old king Henry, address him wisely,
From the king of Scotland their letters then they give him.
    Friar William Dolepene [1] speaks the first,
And said to the king of England : " I am a messenger,
From the king of Scotland I come to inform you :
He is your relation, therefore you must love him much ;
He will serve you in this business, you will not see him delay,
With a thousand knights armed, before an entire month elapses,
With thirty thousand unarmed (so I have heard them reckoned),
330 Who will give your enemies wonderful trouble.
He will not ask the value of a penny from you,
So that you will grant him his rights :
That is Northumberland which he requires first of all,
For nobody has such great reason to challenge it as he has.
Now you see me here in your court, I do not require any future time,
I will leave it to be decided by a single knight ;
And if you will not do it, in order to disinherit him,
Here I return you his homage, I do not seek to conceal it from you."
    When the king of England hears the message
340 Of his cousin of Scotland, of his intention,
He says to his messenger that he will do nothing ;
He does not require, on answering, either stranger or relation :
" Tell the king of Scotland that I am not afraid
Of any war I may have with my son at present,
Neither of the king of France, nor of his people,
Nor the count of Flanders who assails me often.
I will make them enraged and sorry for their war,
And I will give him annoyance, if God allows it me ;
But tell his brother, David, [2] my relation,
350 To come and help me with as many people as he has :
I will give him as much land and as many estates
As to execute all his demands to his satisfaction."
—" Sire," quoth the messenger, " I make a covenant with you for it ;
But give us leave to go in safety."
    Then the messengers set out from Normandy,
Find a good passage, do not delay there,
They traverse England, they come to Albany.
The messengers are wise, they do not care about amusement,
Meet with nobody who does them harm or says any thing bad
360 From the sea of Dover as far as Orkney.
Soon they will tell such a word of war with rage
For which they also shall weep who have not heard it :
" Sire king of Scotland, God save thy baronage,
Thy body and thy courage and thy great retinue !
From the king of England I return as a messenger :

---

[1] "Dolipene," MS. Lincoln. If it were lawful to hazard a conjecture, it would seem that here we ought to read D'Olifent.
[2] David, earl of Huntingdon, was brother of William the Lion. See Dugd. Baron. i. 609.

Now hear his mandate, do not make light of it :
He marvels much at you, that you have madness in your body ;
He considered you a wise man, not of a childish age,
As one whom he loved best, without showing any injury.
You should not have required from him such an outrageous
    deed :
370 You ask him for his land as your inheritance,
As if he were imprisoned as a bird in a cage.
He is neither a fugitive from the land nor become a savage,
But he is king of England in the plains and the woods.
He will not give you for his need in this first stage
Increase of land, this is in his language ;
But will see whether you will show him love and relationship,
How you will behave, as foolish or wise."
Then you might hear those knights, the people young and wild,
380 Swear a strong oath and exhibit courage :
" If you do not war against this king who beards you so,
You must hold neither land nor any lordship ;
But must serve the son of Matilda in bondage."
    Now the king of Scotland hears that his people oppose him ;
He had not Engelram [1] the bishop, the best of his clergy,
Nor earl Waltheof [2] does not venture
To counsel war (he well sees that it is folly),
So that the king himself often opposes him
By the suggestion of those who love folly ;
390 And swears his oath, " God the son of Mary :
The war will not the less take place because of your cowardice.
You have enough in treasure, goods and property :
Defend your land and seek aid for you ;
And, if you will not do so, in all your life
You shall not have of my land the value of a clove of garlick."
    Thus answers him the earl : " Restrain this inclination :
I am your liege-man, so were my relations.
We know nothing of war : therefore I fear.
To begin strife there must be deliberation :
400 You should not trust to foolish enticement,
Nor put faith in the folly of foreign people.
If good can come to you, they will often gain ,
They will not lose much, if it turns out unfortunately for you.
The peasant says in proverb, and says very truly :
' He injures who cannot aid, when the trial comes on.'
Do not imagine that I say it through any fear,
Nor that I shall fail you in war as long as I am living."
    When this counsel was given, the king did not heed it :
The war will still take place, though Albany were lost ;
410 But he wishes to send beyond the sea a spy
To see the situation of the father in Normandy ;
And then afterwards to Flanders, to the son, in whom he trusts,
His letters and messages, to tell him loudly :

[1] Engelram, bishop of Glasgow. Keith's Scottish Bishops, p. 233.
[2] Waltheof, earl of Dunbar, died in 1182. Chronicle of Melrose, ad an.

" How the king his father by word opposes me
And by such a menace as you have heard ;
And if he will keep covenant by pledged faith,
I will not fail to give him aid speedily.
So let him send us from Flanders his Flemings with a navy,
By hundreds and by fifties of those bold people :
420 I will give them the road to the people who war against us.
They will attack the castles by regular siege.
    " William de Saint-Michel will deliver this message,
And Robert de Husevile ; for both are wise :
They have often given proof of ability in need,
They well know in rich court to speak many a language."
    To do this message depart these messengers ;
The king desires it and it is his pleasure, so they do it most willingly.
At Berwick-on-Tyne[1] they find the boatmen,
Who will take to Flanders the wise messengers.
430   Already they have entered barges, and go on the high sea,
And hoist up their sails, and cause the anchor to be weighed ;
They do not care to coast along England :
They are their mortal enemies, whom they used to love.
    When these knights have found their lord
With the king of France, Lewis the emperor,
They deliver their messages gently and without anger,
So that the counts of France hear it well ;
And count Philip is put in such emotion,
The noble warrior speaks before the others.
440   Now speaks count Philip a sensible speech,
Before the court of France ; it was very well heard :
" Keep to the king of Scotland the pledged faith ;
That he may aid you in war, hastily, without delay ;
Destroy your enemies and waste their country,
That by fire and conflagration all may be kindled ;
That he may leave them nothing without, either in forest or in meadow,
Of which they may in the morning have a dinner ;
Then let him besiege their castles with his assembled people :
They shall have no succour nor aid within thirteen leagues.
450   " Thus war should be begun, such is my opinion :
First to destroy the land and then one's enemy.
We will help him from Flanders ere fifteen days come,
By which those of England will be disabled."
    As soon as count Philip finished his attack,
King Lewis of France wills it and agrees to it ;
And says to our messengers : " Soon shall be sealed
The charter that you will take to your country.
Tell the king of Scotland, without any delay,
The land is all his own which he has demanded."
460   When these messengers had come and reached the land,
Then were they quite certain of beginning the war.
Enough you might hear without going far :
" Let us go to take the castle of Wark in England."

[1] Fantome here blunders ; read Berwick-on-Tweed.

Never was born a man so memorable,
Neither Solomon the wise, nor David who wrote the history,
Who did not glory in having such a great victory
As these promised him; but all was vain glory.
Now has the king of Scotland his host prepared
At Caldenle,[1] there they were assembled.
470 The trumpets were what then were loved,
Which afterwards drove them from the land by force.
From Ross and from Moray they have a great host gathered.
Certainly, earl Colbein[2] did not forget himself there.
Lords, the earl of Angus[3] came there with such aid,
More than three thousand Scots he had in his command.
There were so many naked people, I know not what more to tell you,
There came not such a host from Scotland since the time of Elias.
Then came king William to Wark in England,
A castle in the marches which afterwards made him great war,
480 Labour and trouble, and often great opposition;
He inquired from the constable what he meant to do,
Either to hold or give up, which he thought proper.
Roger d'Estutevile[4] was its constable,
Who never liked treason nor to serve the devil;
And saw that his power was of no avail
Against the host of Scotland, which besieges them strongly,
Neither to surrender his castle he should have any terms :
It was no marvel if lord Roger were dismayed.
Then he prays to God the glorious and his mother true :
490 " Such counsel give me that I may preserve my honour,
For the Scots war against me without any respite."
Roger d'Estutevile speaks to his intimate friends,
And says : " Barons, knights, say what you recommend.
See the host of the king of Scotland who has defied us ;
And we shall be scorned within these holds,
We shall have no succour nor help from any of our neighbours."
Then he invokes his lord, Henry the valiant king ;
The tears along his face go falling down :
" Evil was your strength, since now you are powerless !
500 You cannot aid your baron in any way whatever.
I will go to the king of Scotland, asking for a truce,
Forty days space, that I may pass the sea.
If then I cannot succour myself afterwards by right,
You have lost without fail all Northumberland."
Roger d'Estutevile came to speak to the king,
Wise with humility, [and] without doing anything wrong ;
All those of his suite kept themselves in ranks,

<hr>

[1] In MS. Lincoln, Kaledene de gré, which is apparently an error.   There is a
place in Selkirkshire called Caldenlea, where the Calden falls into the Tweed, and
this is most probably the place meant.
[2] Probably Colban, earl of Fife.
[3] Gilibrede, second earl of Angus. Dougl. Peerage of Scotland, i. 62.
[4] Not mentioned in Dugdale's Baronage; but his name occurs as sheriff of
Northumberland from 1170 to 1185 inclusive, in the Pipe Roll for that county,
printed by Hodgson.

And says in his address : " Sire, listen to me.
" Do not do me shame, refrain your ire.
510 Much do I love your welfare, but let not mine suffer.
Forty days space, that I may pass the sea, [give me,] sire,
That I may send beyond sea my letters under wax ;
Or I myself will go there, whichever I please to choose,
And will say to my lord it would be wrong to sing or laugh :
If Jesus does not take care of the people of his empire,
He will not see them, for they will be all delivered to martyrdom."
    Then saw king William Roger in great sorrow,
All Northumberland harassed with woe ;
There is none to oppose him or his vigour :
520 Willingly did he grant the space till the fortieth day.
    Now says Jordan Fantosme [1] that God protected them :
All those of Northumberland who were there,
Were it not for this truce which Roger asked,
Would have been driven from the land by those of Albany ;
But the wise knight who loved his lord
Prepares his messengers, he accoutred himself,
Went to England, asked for help,
So that within his term such a host he brought
That then to the king of Scotland full leave he gave
530 To attack him with his Flemings, and he will wait for them.
    Then says king William : " Hear, my knights.
Throughout Northumberland I will take my way :
There is no one to oppose us, whom should we then fear ?
The bishop of Durham [2] (behold his messenger)
Informs me by his letters he wishes to remain at peace :
Neither from him nor his forces shall we have disturbance,
Of which I can complain to the value of a penny.
Let us go to Alnwick, if you will allow me,
To William de Vesci [3] whom I cannot overcome.
540 If he will give up his father's castle to me,
I will then let him go without loss of limb ;
Or if he will make with me the same agreement
Which the constable of Wark made the day before yesterday,
Without collecting ammunition and without fortifying anything.
Let us go to Warkworth, that I will destroy."
    Then the great host of Albany went to Alnwick ;
But William de Vesci did not forget himself there,
Often calls with love the aid of the Holy Father,
He invokes his lord more than a knight his mistress,
550 And says : " Barons, knights," to those of his bailiwick,
" Wisdom and folly are often good at need :
Now come each of you, tell us your opinion about this,
How we shall manage against the host which defies us."
    Much was the father joyous in his heart
To have begotten a good son, though it was in concubinage :

---

[1] Fantome, MS. Lincoln.   [2] Hugh de Pudsy.
[3] William de Vesci was lord of the castles of Alnwick and Warkworth, both in Northumberland. See Dugd. Baron. i. 92.

Of young William I say it in my language,
Who his father's castle held by vassalage.
The king departed then, made no longer stay there ;
And the former sent for succour his letters and his messenger.
560   Knights and serjeants and the other pillagers
Take and destroy the land next the sea.
They come to Warkworth, do not deign to stop there ;
For weak was the castle, the wall and the trench.
And Roger [1] the son of Richard, a valiant knight,
Had had it in ward ; but he could not guard it.
      Of this Roger the son of Richard I must certainly tell you :
Of Newcastle-on-Tyne was he master and lord ;
He was seized with such boldness and great ire
That he would neither speak of peace to the king of Scotland nor
              laugh.
570   Thither came the king of Scotland with armèd people and naked;
The hills and the valleys dread his coming.
A greater folly than his never was seen,
To the barons of the land it will be very dearly sold :
He will give them, before his departure, such a discomfiture
He will not leave them outside the castle an ox to their plough.
      But the barons are devoted to their lord,
They care as little for their property as does a wild beast ;
They prefer dying with honour rather than suffer shame
[And] abandon their natural lord, though they lose their lands.
580 They will endure and wait : they do so wisely ;
But they will not surrender their castles though they suffered great
              damage.
      Well sees the king of Scotland that he will never succeed
In conquering Newcastle-on-Tyne without stratagem ;
And say his counsellors : " Wrongly do you hang your head.
[Before succour comes to them, they all will be in despair ;] [2]
But warn the host to be ready in the morning ;
Go conquer Carlisle, of which we spoke.
[Robert de Vaus [3] will never have such a good sable,
Nor eat meat, nor drink such wine,
590 When he sees so many fine shields, so many Poitevin helmets,
But he will wish to be a bishop on the chess-board."]
      Thus said king William : " Then may I be cursed,
Excommunicated by priest, shamed and discomfited,
If to the castle of Odinel [4] I give any terms or respite !
But I will entirely put an end to his joy and his delight.
Earl Henry [5] my father loved and reared him ;
But at length he will say that it was a misfortune to see me,

---

[1] This baron is often mentioned in the Pipe Rolls, 14 Hen. II. Concerning
him, see Hodgson's Magnus Rotulus Pipæ, pp. xii. xiv.
    [2] This line is wanting in the Lincoln MS., as are also lines 588—591.
    [3] See concerning him, Dugd. Baron. i. 525.
    [4] Odinel de Umfraville's castle was that of Prudhoe in Northumberland.
Dugd. Baron. i. 504.
    [5] Henry, the father of king William, was the son of David I., king of
Scotland.

For he in whom he trusts will be of a very little use to him.
[He makes him a refusal of his assistance."] [1]
600   There the king of Scotland made his earls, his barons,
Pitch his pavilions, his tents and his marquees ;
And said to his baronage : " Lords, what shall we do there ?
As long as Prudhoe stands, we will never have peace."
Thus say the Flemings : " We will destroy it,
Or wrongly you will give us pay and provisions."
And said the other party : " Never will we speak of it,
We will never consent to his making any enterprise ;
But let him go forward to conquer, and we will help him.
Northumberland is ours, when we come back."
610   — " Sire, king of Scotland," say his counsellors,
" Of all your rights Carlisle is the most difficult [to secure] ;
And since the young king is willing to give you all,
Go and conquer the capital, we advise you thus ;
And if Robert de Vaus will not give the chief town,
From the old high tower you must have him thrown.
Lay siege to it, and then make your great assembled host
To swear not to stir from it
Till you have seen the city on fire,
The master-wall pulled down with your pickaxes of steel,
620 Himself fastened to a high gallows.
Then you will see Robert de Vaus slinking away ;
As far as I know, you will not find him so bold
That he will be able to resist you long by force."
And said king William : " If God will aid us,
This counsel is advisable, so let us execute it."
In the night he makes his watchmen watch his host,
Till the following morning at dawn when the day appeared clear.
When he made his trumpets sound to put the host in motion ;
And the serjeants and esquires take down the tents.
630   King William goes with his great baronage ;
But before they return to their wild country,
They will have made such damage among the English of England
That a thousand will leave their heads there for their own hostage.
For they are fierce in war and of very rash courage :
This is quite evident to those whom they find in their way.
Those who are caught in plain or in wood
Will never tell stories to any of their lineage.
    Well knew the king of Scotland to make war upon his enemies,
And often in war to grieve and injure [them] ;
640 But he was too much accustomed to listen to new advice.
He cherished, loved and held foreigners dear ;
His own people he would never love,
Who should of right advise him and his kingdom
This appeared soon, presently you shall hear me speak of it,
What happened of his war through evil counsellors.
The king makes his people get ready ;
To those within he will give a complete assault.

Great was the noise at the beginning of the fight,
The swords clash, and the steel crashes,
650 [Scarcely a hauberk or helmet remained whole.] [1]
That day those within were knights,
With their swords they make many a shield shattered,
They leave many of them stretched near the wall
Who had no leisure to get up again.
Henceforth those within must help [themselves],
Endure the battle and damage the shields,
Hold and contend for their barbican :
No coward could be useful to them.
At the gate there was a great attack,
660 On both sides great was the fury.
Then you might see so many bleeding knights,
So many good vassals in bad humour ;
The swords clash and intermingle.
Robert de Vaus defended himself bravely ;
The son of Odard [2] was not at all behindhand,
For his lord he behaved himself most daringly
In standing against so many people :
Forty thousand, if Fantosme [3] does not lie.
There is none who does not hate him mortally.
670   Oh! God! what sorrow for gentle king William!
From king Henry he will have such mortal blame ;
This grieves me, by the illustrious saint James !
For a nobler man never governed a realm.
    Fantosme says and assures to us well
That he would not think any day of his life
To fight Henry of Normandy,
The son of Matilda who has the hardy countenance ;
But by counsel and by evil envy
One may make a wise man commit a great folly.
680   But since he had undertaken the thing thus,
He could not leave it so through great cowardice.
He orders peace to be kept towards the holy church,
On those who infringe it he executes cruel justice ;
But that is not worth to him a single clove of garlic :
The rascally people, (whom may the Lord God curse !)
The Welsh, who wish for booty,
And the Scots, who are in Albany,
Have no faith in God the Son of Mary ;
They break open the churches and commit great robberies.
690   The barons put themselves to great trouble
Who held their estates from the sovereign king ;
For their lord they have great sorrow certainly :
His enemies have given them a present.
If God and Mary Magdalen do not think of it,
Great war they will have which will be very severe to them.

[1] This line is wanting in the Lincoln MS.
[2] John Fitz-Odard is mentioned in the Northumberland Pipe Roll, 14 Hen. II.
See Hodgson's Magnus Rotulus Pipæ, p. xiv.   [3] "Fantome" MS. Lincoln.

The land which was so full of such prosperity
Is now spoiled and destitute of all riches;
There is no drink but spring water
Where they used to have beer in the week.
700 And all is done by the king of Albany,
By his counsel and by his great folly;
But now there arises to him great loss infallibly,
He will not depart without having shame.
Those of the castle will have speedy aid:
So fares it with people who in the Lord God trust.
    Hear, lords, what happens from too great daring,
What happened to them from savage Scotland.
Fine was the weather without any bad storm;
The king of Scotland was of bold courage,
710 Good knight and of great valour.
Before him came wandering a messenger,
A canon was he, and knew the language;
Hastily he related to him his complaint.
    The king was in his pavilion;
The warders near and around,
His chamberlains and his private friends,
There where the messenger delivered to them such a speech
By which they were afterwards excited to contention.
The messenger told them the whole,
720 How he had seen the armed people,
The great pride of the chevaliers
Who would assault him before sunrise.
" He of Lucy, the wise, the sensible,
Before midnight will be joined with our men.
Take care thereof, for God of majesty,
That you are not disgraced nor shamed.
All the best of your relations
Come with him, every one has sworn to him.
Trust to advice, the best is given to you.
730 To Roxburgh go in safety.
If you delay any longer,
A bad song will be sung of you.
Never did Thibault de Balesgué [1] give

[1] "The romance, to which Fantosme alludes here, was well known in England. In a certificate or memoir concerning some books found, in the third year of Edward I.'s reign, we find this mention of it: 'Le Romaunce Willeame de Orenges et Tabaud de Arable.' *Formulare Anglicanum*, p. 12, No. xxiii. A copy of it was bequeathed by Guy Beauchamp, earl of Warwick, to the abbey of Bordesley in Worcestershire, May 1st, 34 Edward I. or III. See our *Tristan*, vol. i. p. cxxi. l. 2.
    "Fantosme's allusion, and the following lines taken from a poem of the twelfth century, show its antiquity:
                Mais une merveille veoit
                Qui poïst faire grant paor
                Au plus hardi combateor
                De toz ices que nos savons,
                Se fust *Thiebauz li Esclavons*
                Ou Opiniax ou Fernaguz, etc.
(*Le Roman d'Érec et d'Enide*, MS. of the Royal Library, No. 7498⁴, Cangé, 26, fol. 41 verso, col. 2. l. 26.)"—*Michel's Note*.

So bad a check to the natives of France
As those hardened ones of the south will give you,
If you and they encounter each other."
The king hears him, and is very angry,
Without delay swore by saint Andrew :
" We stop here quite secure ;
740 Battle will not be refused them.
A brave man ought certainly to conquer his inheritance.
My ancestors of the kingdom of Scotland
Held that estate in quietness.
By this Lord whom they implore on foot !
And I will hold it from the king to whom I am pledged,
The son of the father who has given me my rights ;
As long as I live I will not lose a single foot of it."
He would have already well addressed his host,
When a counsel is given him by his men :
750 As he wished to be still honoured,
He should leave the siege and depart of his own free will.
So he did indeed, nor stayed longer there,
By none of his men were the reins drawn.
To Roxburgh, where they were before,
He went by night like one who was in haste ;
Not a single one of his host lagged behind,
Who did not go away through very great cowardice,
Without any attack having been made upon them
Or being shouted at or damaged in any thing.
760   Robert de Vaus gained in this chase,
He earned great wealth from these fugitives ;
But, whoever is sorry for it or bears any ill will to him,
He will strengthen his place with their property.
Bends his foot and extends his talons,
Thanks God and prays that He will not hate him.
    Now the great host of England rides secure.
Sir Richard de Lucy, no better needs be sought for,
Well assists his lord to maintain his war,
And he knows at need to ask for truces and peace
770 Where he sees force and it is necessary to ask for them.
    He rides in the land destroyed and wasted :
That is Northumberland which was already renowned.
From here to the passes of Spain there was not such a country
Nor more fruitful, nor people more honoured ;
Now it is in great famine, it has become annihilated,
If by the king of England aid is not given.
He sighs and thinks how it is decayed,
And curses the war for having already begun ;
Then he thinks in his heart, if the Lord God pleases,
780 By him and his forces it will be soon avenged,
And by the good men who are of the country,
Who desire greatly to revenge their sufferings.
    Sir Humphrey de Bohun [1] was of very great cleverness,

[1] See Dugd. Baron. i. 179.

As soon as he can spur he goes from the chief-justice:
It is lord Richard de Lucy whom every body prizes.
He did not wish to provoke the king of Scotland in any way,
For a messenger of his tells him news:
He had come to the land, who will lay siege to them.
The earl of Leicester has thus undertaken the thing
790 With Flemings and with French and with people towards Friseland,
He will turn England wholly at his command.
" God!" quoth Richard de Lucy, " what great distress I am in!
If the king of Scotland knew what is doing;
We should have neither peace nor truce for all the wealth of France;
And he ought not to do it, unless he were a great child."
He rides and spurs, and has in his heart heaviness;
But before he could succeed to speak in the hearing
Of the king of Albany or do his business
Had lord Humphrey de Bohun who boldly advances
800 Caused to the king of Scotland the loss of Berwick.
     Lord Humphrey de Bohun was of very great consequence;
The barons of Northumberland are his companions in it;
They burnt all Berwick with fire and firebrands
And a great part of the surrounding country,
For they appear in their marches cruel as lions;
But lord Richard de Lucy does not care for such speech.
And says in his language: " Sir Humphrey de Bohun,
[The barons of Northumberland are his companions in it] [1]
Ah! if God does not take care, we shall certainly lose.
810   " Sir Humphrey de Bohun," quoth Richard de Lucy,
[Who did not go away through very great cowardice,
Without any attack having been made upon them
Or being shouted at or damaged in any thing.
Robert de Vaus gained in this chase] [2]
 " Let us go to the king of Scotland to cry him mercy
To hold peace and truce to our king Henry.
The most of England have all failed him.
Know you the news that we have heard?
The earl of Leicester has ill-treated us all:
820 He has arrived in North Wales,[3] you may be certain of it,
And has taxed the land as if he was sheriff of it,
As far as Dunwich by force he got it."
     Now is Humphrey de Bohun angry in his heart:
" Sir Richard de Lucy, your age will now appear;
And if you are now, as they say, so wise,
Go in haste to the king of Scotland, conceal from him this damage.
If he knows this news he will be of a very fierce courage.
That the earl has arrived and succeeded in passing,
He will not give you his truce, unless he has madness in his body;

---

[1] This line, evidently a repetition of line 802, does not occur in the Lincoln MS.
[2] Another careless repetition of the lines 757—760. This mistake is not found in the Lincoln MS.
[3] Arwelle, MS. Lincoln, obviously the correct reading, as Orwell harbour in Sussex is the point indicated. See further, line 841.

830 I will go back, it will be for his damage.
   If God is willing and agrees, I will efface the outrage.
   Wrongly they had arrived from Flanders the wild."
     Now has Richard de Lucy done as a sensible [man],
   He has from the king of Scotland all he had asked
   Of truces for Northumberland till about summer;
   And lord Humphrey de Bohun is gone back
   And many a gentle knight in England born;
   They will be in a short time with Flemings acquainted.
   You have heard it well, the little and the great,
840 That earl Robert is gone so far forward
   That he has arrived in Suffolk,[1] [and] goes taxing the land;
   As far as Dunwich all moves by his command,
   Many a gentleman of Flanders goes this day following him:
   Whereat the king of England had afterwards a great joy.
   Earl Hugh Bigod[2] has taken his messengers,
   And announces to those of Dunwich that he is their friend,
   That they should take part with the earl, and they should have play
       and amusement,
   Or that they would lose their heads who are still living;
   And those have answered him that wrongly counsel would be taken
       about it,
850 On the contrary they will sell themselves very dear to their enemies.
     Surely you have heard it in proverb:
   " He who commits treason to his lawful lord
   Or any felony by which he suffer injury,
   To have bad recompense must not doubt;
   And he who loyally serves him is much to be esteemed."
   So did the people of Dunwich, of whom you hear me speak.
   The earl of Leicester wished to besiege them,
   And swore his oath as he was accustomed,
   If the burghers and the peers did not surrender themselves to him,
860 There should not escape a man without death or injury;
   And these answer him with emulation:
   " Confounded be he who dreads you to the amount of a penny!
   Still living is the good lawful king,
   Who will very soon bring your war to an end.
   As long as we can live and stand on our feet,
   We will not surrender the town from fear of any assault."
   The earl of Leicester began to be angry,
   And erects the gallows to frighten them;
   Then causes to arm in haste serjeants and esquires,
870 To assault the town vigorously he resolved to do what he could.
   That day you might have seen burghers, very valiant knights,
   Sally out to their fortifications; each knows his business,
   Some to shoot with bows, others to cast darts;
   The strong help the feeble often to repose.
   There was within the town neither maid or woman

    [1] " Arivez en Sufolke," MS. Durham. " Erwelle, Suffoke," MS. Lincoln See
note to line 820.
    [2] Hugh Bigod, earl of Norfolk. Dugd. Baron. i. 132.

Who did not carry a stone to the palisade to cast.
　So did the people of Dunwich defend themselves,
As these verses speak which are here written ;
And so brave were the great and the little
880 That earl Robert went away quite scorned.
　The earl of Leicester is of very great valour,
Towards the people of Dunwich he found no love ;
Neither assault nor vassal could be of any use to him,
Nor serjeant nor esquire, whom those might fear.
He and the earl set about returning,
Till the morrow at dawn, when he saw the day appear.
　He called his constables, and said to them in hearing :
" Cause your men to mount, delay will be wrong.
I will go to Norwich, if God gives me power,
890 To see their business, what is their countenance."
And those do not delay to do the deed ;
Soon might you see in haste displayed many a sleeve,
Many a pennon of silk borne on fine lance,
And many a good gentle vassal, many a man of great valour.
　If any wish to hear the truth how Norwich was taken,
I was not in the country when it was besieged :
A Lorrain traitor betrayed it, therefore it was surprised.
None can guard himself against treason in any guise,
Except only king Henry, who punishes the cruel
900 By the power of the Creator and the prayer of holy church ;
He never made pretence to keep peace according to his power,
And may God, who never lied, preserve him in his service !
　Jordan Fantosme first wanted to give himself up,
On all the reliques an oath to swear,
There is no clerk in all the world, ever so clever in recording
His lesson in his book, or in speaking of any art,
Who could tell me or can mention
A land which from hence to Montpellier
Is worth that of Norfolk, of which you hear me speak,
910 More honoured knights or more hospitable,
Or merrier dames to give largely,
Except the town of London, of which nobody knows its peer ;
To the barons of the town none could be compared.
Never in this war you heard speak of any,
Let him be ever so rich in land, who dared besiege them,
Or point towards them the finger even in thought,
Who had not a sore recompense in lieu of his pay.
Gentle king of England, just imagine
How you ought to love London and the barons ;
920 For never did they fail their lawful lord,
But were always the first at his need.
They had enough of messengers from Flanders beyond the sea,
Who promised to give them great honours.
Your own son, whom you should love much,
Since by nature he has begun to be reconciled,
Asked them by letters and by his messengers

To help him to war against his father,
On such condition as you will hear me name,
That all the days of his life he would hold them so dear,
930 Would love and cherish, and much would give them ;
But they would not do it nor even consent to it
To chase or exile you from your kingdom.
    Therefore you ought to love, honour and cherish them,
And at their great need their loyalty recompense,
Since for any promise they would never swerve ;
But to love you as they could was their pleasure.
Gentle king of England, do my desire ;
Love those who wish to serve you in loyalty.
There should not to the young king come any harm
940 (Since by natural affection he has begun to repent)
From bringing foreign people to injure his own
Who after the days of his father are to support him.
Before this century comes to an end,
Many adventures may happen.
Never had you such a war to sustain,
But your son had a greater ; now let him think of nourishing his
    people.
    The earl of Leicester does not cease to waste
The land of Norfolk, of which you hear me speak ;
He could not in Normandy injure king Henry :
950 Therefore he wanted to embroil England as much as he could.
He has with him Flemings by hundreds and by thousands.
Earl Hugh the Bigod wished to aid him altogether ;
And the earl of Ferrieres,[1] a simple knight
(He had better kiss and embrace a fair lady
Than with a hammer of war strike a knight),
Informs him by his letters he may go secure
Throughout all England, he will have no disturbance there.
The earl tells him those who wish to war :
It is the king of Scotland whom he first named,
960 And lord David his brother who is much to be prized,
And lord Roger of Mowbray [2] who was always a warrior.
" He will come to succour you where you want it.
All the land is on fire : think of moving.
The old king of England will have need of his people ;
He is in great difficulty, so we must praise God :
Never in his life will he pass the sea,
But will have lost Normandy by passing.
If you could ride to Leicester,
Before Easter came you might go
970 As far as the Tower of London, there would be no disturbance.
The good city of York is lord Roger's,
Throughout all Yorkshire he proclaims himself lord.
There are within my country scarcely any knights,
Whom I will not kill outright, if I have not their aid."
    —" Oh ! God !" thus said the earl, " how enraged I could be now !

---

[1] Robert earl of Ferrers. Dugd. Baron. i. 219.   [2] Id. i. 122.

I have been too long waiting to help my lord
And to revenge myself on the old king his father and for my injuries.
Shall I hear, lords knights, any one of you speak?
To do this business who will dare advise me?"
980 —" Yes, sir," quite boldly answered him his wife.
" Lord God forbid, who is lawful king,
That you for Humphrey de Bohun should give up this journey,
Either for the earl of Arundel[1] or for his fair speech!
The English are great boasters, they do not know how to fight;
Better they know with large cups to drink and act the glutton.
The earl of Gloucester[2] is much to be feared;
But he has your sister for wife and companion:
For all the wealth of France he would not begin
To commit any outrage from which you would have disturbance."
990 —" Dame," so said the earl, " now I hear you speak;
Your counsel I must follow, for much I love you.
—Sir Hugh del Chastel,[3] will you grant it?
If you were at Leicester in danger,
Of all the men of England you need not be afraid;
But might often cause them great trouble."
And said Hugh del Chastel: " There is nothing to do but go."
Soon you might hear shouting very loud
Between Flemings from Flanders and French and Pohier:[4]
" We have not come to this country to dwell,
1000 But to destroy king Henry the old warrior,
And to have his wool, which we desire."
Lords, that is the truth: the most were weavers,
They did not know how to bear arms like knights.
    But for this they had come, to have gain and war;
For there is no place on earth more hospitable than Saint-Edmund's.
    Now listen, lords barons, to God's great vengeance,
Which he poured down on Flemings and on the people of France.
The earl of Leicester was of great power;
But he was in heart too youthful and childish
1010 When through England he wished to go publicly,
Committing his robberies without having disturbance,
And makes his wife take arms, carry shield and lance.
His great folly will take hard birth.
Saint-Edmund's had knights of very great power,
It arms them in haste without any delay:
It was Walter Fitz-Robert, of whom you hear speak,
Who first encountered the Flemings and put them into a bad way.
Indeed, the earl of Arundel (he never loved delay)
Thither came with the train, whom saint Edmund prosper!
1020 Sir Humphrey de Bohun caused them annoyance;
Soon you will see them come to blows, there is no other separation.

[1] William de Albini, concerning whom see Dugd. Baron. i. 118.
[2] Id. i. 535.
[3] This French nobleman is frequently mentioned by Hoveden, William of Newborough, and Benedictus Abbas.
[4] See Du Cange, under the word "Poheri." These were the inhabitants of a small principality called Poix.

The earl of Leicester stopped short,
And saw the armed people who came approaching them :
" Sir Hugh del Chastel, now here come forward,
And all your company, the little and the great.
By my conscience ! we will not go farther,
We will accept battle very hard and very heavy.
Behold hauberks and helmets against the sun shining ;
But now be knights, for God's sake I command you.
1030 Woe to the body of the man who first runs away,
That it may never be said in a proverb that we are recreants."
The earl of Arundel is of great pride,
And says to Humphrey de Bohun : " Now let us go and attack them
In honour of God and saint Edmund, who is a true martyr."
Answers Roger le Bigod : " Quite at your pleasure !
I never in my life had so great a desire for anything
As to destroy the Flemings, whom I see coming here."
    It was Walter Fitz-Robert who spurred on the first,
Now may the omnipotent King be his aid !
1040 And goes to attack the Flemings very furiously ;
And they resist him, who fear him not.
They were more than he by thousands and by hundreds,
So they force him back with his people ;
But he did not delay to seek vengeance :
Woe to them that they saw England, all will be sorry for it.
He encountered the earl, and said to him harshly :
" You are the man of my lord, be not slow ;
See his enemies going to his destruction.
Spur on, sir earl, along with us."
1050 And this he swore by God's lance, (that was his oath,)
Woe to Robert that he brought from Flanders such people.
Then you might see the earl who drew himself up proudly,
And lord Roger le Bigod who undertakes great deeds.
Nor did lord Hugh de Creissy [1] fail them at all ;
But before they could fall upon them at their pleasure,
Humphrey de Bohun had retained more than a hundred.
    Certainly well does Robert Fitz-Bernard [2] perform,
Of this foreign people he makes a wonderful clearance ;
Neither can Flemings or Lombards assist themselves :
1060 The wool of England they gathered very late.
Upon their bodies descend crows and buzzards,
Who carry away the souls to the fire which ever burns.
There the priest of Suart will say mass for them ;
It would be better for them in Flanders to hang by a rope.
    The Flemings would have been very brave, if God were their aid ;
But they had not deserved it for their great robberies.
The earl of Leicester saw their company to his misfortune,
And lord Hugh del Chastel will not rejoice in it :
They are in the midst of the crowd, feeble, without aid.
1070 My lady the countess has entered the way,

---

[1] Dugd. Baron. i. 703.
[2] Mentioned in Hoved. Annal. A.D. 1172, fol. 302, b.

And met with a ditch where she was almost drowned,
In the midst of the mud her rings she forgets ;
Never will they be found in all her life.
   The wife of the earl wished to drown herself intentionally,
When Simon de Vahull¹ set about lifting her up :
" Lady, come away with me, give up that idea ;
Thus it fares in war, to lose or to gain."
Then began earl Robert to be strongly affected
When he saw his wife taken, he had good reason to be angry,
1080 And saw his companions slain by hundreds and by thousands :
The colour began to change in his face.
   Lord Humphrey de Bohun and the earl of Arundel
Have detained the earl and Hugh del Chastel,
And lord Roger le Bigod was this day newly arrived ;
To him and to Hugh de Creissy this deed seemed very fine.
There was in the country neither villager nor clown
Who did not go to destroy the Flemings with fork and flail.
With nothing meddled the armed knights
But only with knocking them down, and the villagers with killing them ;
1090 By fifteens, by forties, by hundreds and by thousands
By main force they make them tumble into the ditches.
If God did a miracle there, it is not to be wondered at ;
For never in my life I heard speak of any man,
However bold he might be in arms, however valiant a knight,
If he wanted to war against king Henry,
And even those of England desired to aid him,
Who did not end by getting the worst of it.
   After earl Robert was taken and defeated,
All England was somewhat more secure.
1100 All the Flemings of Flanders met with hard luck,
None of the king's enemies feels secure of anything.
   Earl David of Scotland, whatever may be said of him,
Was a most gentle warrior, so God bless me ;
For never by him was robbed holy church or abbey,
And none under his orders would have injured a priest.
It was in May after April when the grass has grown green,
That David came from Scotland with proud company,
[Having] become his brother's man, in the presence of his baronage,
On giving him all Lennox all the days of his life,
1110 Besides the honour of Huntingdon ; he has pledged his faith for it :
That and much more he will give him, provided he assist him
To make war on king Henry, the duke of Normandy.
   Now has David of Scotland to England come
With hauberks and with helmets and with fine painted shields.
Those of Leicester sent him greeting,
And say how it has happened to their lord :
Now let him come to defend them, and he will be well received ;
By him and by his force will the castle be held.
Certainly, to Bertram de Verdun² it will be very dearly sold ;
1120 If it fall into their hands, he will be very angry.

¹ Dugd. Baron. i. 504.   ² Id. i. 471.

Now hear, lords, of the earl how he was taken:
He had in Huntingdon left some of his friends,
He was in Leicester exceedingly powerful;
To those of Nottingham it will be worse every day.
   Those of Northampton were of great valour;
But lord David of Scotland put them to great difficulty:
He could not have tribute from them for love,
So he made a hostile expedition against the burghers one day.
Certainly, whoever will listen, I will tell him the truth of it.
1130 Well did the earl and all his companions.
   Exceedingly well did the knights who came from the castle.
Lord Bertram de Verdun was there this day newly arrived,
He had fine arms and a horse very fleet,
From many who jousted he the prize carried off;
And lord David of Scotland did there his best,
He carried off such a booty as seemed to him very fine.
   David in England warred very well;
But the war turned out badly to the king of Scotland:
By his evil counsellors he undertook to do such a thing
1140 From which at the end came to him very great misfortune.
David was very wise, and was also amiable,
And protected holy Church, for never did he wish to wrong
A priest or canon who knew grammar,
Nor nun of abbey would he displease on any account.
   It was after Easter, I ought to remember well,
That the king of Scotland began to return
Towards Northumberland to waste and injure.
Oh, God! what great damage I saw befall them!
When the king of Scotland came to attack Wark,
1150 On whatever side he wished to assault,
Roger d'Estutevile had prepared himself there for it.
Woe to Fantosme,[1] if you ever hear me lie!
And if I lie to you, you may well hear this,
How Roger laboured to serve his lord.
   Hear of the king of Scotland how he warred,
When he departed from Wark how he proposed:
He prepared at night a great number of chevaliers,
To the castle of Bamborough[2] immediately despatched them.
I well knew the baron who conducted and led them;
1160 I will not speak of him, for much has he lost by it.
   This assembled host will do wonderful damage.
Now would to Jesus the son of holy Mary
That the poor people had been then warned of it,
Who in their beds are sleeping and know nothing of it!
It was still morning when the dawn cleared up,
When these chevaliers armed themselves, the fierce company;
The town of Belford[3] was first attacked.

[1] Above this word a contemporary hand has written "auctor libri" in the Lincoln manuscript.
[2] The castle of Bamborough, situated on the sea-coast of Northumberland.
[3] A small town in the north of the county last mentioned.

Over all the country they scattered themselves :
Some run to towns to commit their folly,
1170 Some go to take sheep in their folds,
Some go to burn the towns, I cannot tell you more :
Never will such great destruction be heard spoken of.
Then might you see peasants and Flemings who tie them,
And lead them in their cords like heathen people.
Women fly to the minster, each was ravished
Naked without clothes, she forgets there her property.
    Ah, God ! why did William de Vesci not know it,
Roger d'Estuteville, the others also ?
The booty would have been rescued, nor would they have failed in it ;
1180 But they knew it not, certainly it grieves me.
They burnt the country ; but God was a friend
To those gentle peasants who were defenceless,
For the Scots were not their mortal enemies :
They would have beaten, slain and ill-treated them all.
    Very great was the booty which the royalists carry away,
They came to Berwick on Tyne [1] to their lodgings,
They have joy enough for that and much amusement ;
For they are rich in cattle, oxen and horses
And in fine cows, sheep and lambs,
1190 In clothes and money, in bracelets and rings.
    Then sent the king of Scotland for his knights,
The earls of his land, all the best warriors ;
To Wark he wished to lay siege by his good counsellors,
He wished to have the castle by Flemings and archers,
By good stone-bows, by his engines very strong
And by his slingers and his cross-bow-men.
    Will you hear of Roger how he behaved himself ?
He was not the least dismayed when this host came to him :
He had in his train knights more than twenty,
1200 Certainly, the best serjeants that ever baron retained.
The host was marvellous, of great chivalry,
Of Flemings and Border-men fierce was the company.
Roger d'Estuteville has garrisoned his house,
He does not fear their siege the value of a clove of garlick :
He has a very gentle baronage to whom he trusts much,
And to exhort them well he did not forget.
By a Monday morning were equipped
Those who shall assault the castle, Flemings they were named,
Then you might see bucklers seized and shields buckled on,
1210 The port-cullis assaulted, as you may soon hear.
By wonderful daring they came to the ditches ;
Those who were inside did not forget themselves ;
They soon struck each other and were so mingled together
That I never saw a better defence in these two kingdoms.
The Flemings were daring and very courageous,
And the other much enraged in their fortress.
Soon you might see serjeants and Flemings so mingled,

[1] A repetition of the mistake already noticed at line 428.

Shields and bucklers broken, pennons displayed,
Flemings turning back from the port-cullises, wounded;
1220 Some were carried from the port-cullises by others;
Never will they cry Arras! [until] dead they are and buried.
   Long lasted this assault; but little succeeded:
Certainly king William did not cease to lose.
Roger d'Estuteville exhorted his men,
By very gentle words he addressed and harangued them:
"Gentle barons companions, by God who formed you!
Do not speak basely, and we will not do so;
If they assault us, God will defend us.
They do wrong to king Henry, for he has done no harm.
1230   "Shoot not your arrows forth but on great occasions;
We know not their intentions and nothing of their thoughts.
They have wide ways and roads and paths,
Wine and beer, drink, food,
And are rich in arms and in fleet steeds;
And we are here within, serjeants and soldiers:
If we have victuals, let us keep them willingly.
Spare your arms, I say that to you, archers;
But when you see need and great complete assaults,
Then defend your heads like gentle chevaliers."
1240   Roger d'Estuteville exhorted thus the people,
And the king of Scotland was greatly enraged.
When he saw his serjeants die and often fail
And saw that he was not gaining ground, he was grieved in heart;
And said to his chevaliers in his great irritation:
   "Make your stone-bow come hastily;
It will soon break the gate, if the engineer lies not;
And we shall take the outer fortification without any delay."
   Hear, lords, of the stone-bow how it went on:
The first stone which it ever cast at them,
1250 The stone was scarcely parted from the sling
When it knocked one of their knights to the ground.
Were it not for his armour and the shield which he had,
To none of his lineage had he ever returned;
Much must he hate the engineer who contrived that for them,
And the king of Scotland who lost more by it.
   Then said king William a marvellous joke:
"Certainly this deed seems to me very costly
Rage possesses my heart and wrath so hideous,
I had rather be taken quite alive before Toulouse."
1260   It is no marvel if he has heaviness in his heart:
Woe that he saw Flemings of Flanders and then the king of
      France;
He knows well the truth at last and without mistake:
That he has lost king Henry without any remedy,
And cannot injure him by buckler or lance
Nor by engine of war, from which he may have much harm.
When the stone-bow failed him, he ordered up the other:
He fain would burn the castle, he knows not what to do better;

But Jesus the glorious, the Creator of all things,
Turned against the king of Scotland the wind very contrary,
1270 And to Roger the baron it began much to please.
    Now he has such great gladness, in his life he never had more.
    Then said king William : " Let us raise this siege ;
I see my people destroyed and the mischief which cuts us off.
Certainly, this affair grieves me strongly at heart.
Roger d'Estuteville has found us out."
    The king of Scotland made his host watch in the night,
Until the following day at dawn when daylight appeared clear,
When he assembled all his earls and barons :
" Gentle barons, knights, now hear me speak :
1280 Let us raise this siege, we can make nothing of it ;
But we have great loss by it : think of restoring it.
Kindle the fire, burn these huts,
Collect and fold your tents and pavilions,
And cause all my host to go Roxburgh."
Then you might see these merchants coming and going,
Unpitching the pavilions, and unfolding the tents,
Through this host of Scotland making great noise :
Of his great discomfiture he might well remember.
King William departed, who wished to go.
1290 Now they set the huts on fire and burn them.
Very great was the noise, that is not to be concealed from you,
Which in this host servants and esquires make.
Roger d'Estuteville was no coward,
Nor fearful in war, nor a base knight ;
Never of a wiser man did you hear speak,
Nor of more steady nor of more gentle warrior.
When he saw this assembled host going towards Roxburgh,
To his gentle baronage he began to speak :
" Say nothing wrong ; for God's sake ! let it be,
1300 Neither cry at nor hoot these people of Scotland ;
But God our Father we must all praise :
When he from the king of Scotland and from his host so wild
Has preserved us our lives, we ought to thank Him.
    " To play or to amuse yourselves I forbid not ;
And when you see the king and his assembled host depart,
Then shout your joy each for himself ;
I shall do the same, so that it shall be heard.
The son injures the father, who opposes him so."
Then might you hear the cornets sounding by ranks :
1310 There were no reproaches, nor taunting words said ;
But songs and choruses and friendly salutations ;
Of horns and trumpets very fine was the accord.
    Roger d'Estuteville is glad at heart,
Well ought he to be so, do not wonder at it ;
For the king of Scotland has left him his own :
He has, thank God, neither lost nor won,
And has none of his followers slain or injured,
Knight or serjeant in the body wounded

For whom he should have to give a coined denier
1320 To a physician of Salerno to be treated for it.
　　Lords, in such disgraceful manner departed king William
From Wark, and for that siege he will still have blame.
He has such great wrath in his heart that he almost faints from it.
Then has sworn an oath, saint Andrew and saint James,
He will not give up the war though he were to lose his kingdom.
　　Behold Robert de Mowbray, who well knew war ;
To his two eldest sons had left his land,
His castles, his domains, and they knew what to do.
He came to the king of Scotland to beg and to request
330 That he would fight quite securely, for that it was the truth
That there was not on earth any one who could oppose him.
Now has the king such joy, never in his life had he more ;
Never would he draw back from doing wrong.
　　In the night was the counsel taken how they should act :
To royal Carlisle in the morning they shall go,
No one disputes it ; but now they shall begin,
They will never cease to look for their injury.
　　Now is Roger de Mowbray with the king of Albany
To make war according to his power, with strength and in aid,
340 So is lord Adam de Porz[1] with great chivalry ;
They were the best warriors known to be in existence.
They had been once so ; but they little know
That God will not long consent to their folly.
Away goes king William with his great gathered host
Towards Carlisle the fair, the strong garrisoned city.
Lord Roger de Mowbray and his chivalry
And lord Adam de Porz joins himself to his Border-men.
The earls of Scotland lead the hated people,
Who never had any repugnance to do fiendish things.
1350 They make such progress, I know not what more to tell you,
That they could see Carlisle full of beauty;
The sun illuminates the walls and turrets.
He who has a merry banner, gladly displays it ;
And the trumpets sound in every rank :
You might hear noise in the shuddering city ;
But lord Robert de Vaus gently begs them
Not to be dismayed nor act cowardly;
For, if God keeps his life safe and sound,
He fears not at all this host nor the king of Albany.
1360 　The king summons Roger and Adam to council,
Walter de Berkeley,[2] who was one of his retainers :
" Now behold, noble knights, much gentle preparation ;
You cannot count the white nor the red,
So many are the banners dancing in the sun !
　　" Go to Robert, say that I send him this message :—
Surrender me the castle this very moment :
He will have no succour from any living man,
And the king of England will never more be his defender ;

---

[1] See Dugd. Baron. i. 463.　　　　　[2] See Chalmers' Caledonia, i. 523.

And if he will not do so, swear well to him
1370 He shall lose his head for it and his children shall die.
I will not leave him a single friend or relation
Whom I will not exile, if he does not execute my command."
Now go the barons demanding the truce,
They go to Robert de Vaus where he was ;
He was dressed in a hauberk, leaning on a battlement,.
And held in his hand a keen sword
With a sharp edge, he handled it gently ;
And saw the messenger who called him,
From him and his men asking the truce.
1380 And he answered him : " Friend, what is it you want ?
You might soon leave there the little and the great."
And said the messenger : " That is not courteous :
A messenger carrying his message should not be
Insulted or ill-treated ; he may say what he likes."
And said Robert de Vaus : " Now come nearer,
Say your pleasure ; be afraid of nothing."
Lords, in such way as this did the messenger speak
To Robert, who is the chief, and to all the baronage :
" Sir Robert de Vaus, you are valiant and wise.
1390 I am the king's messenger, he is my protector ;
He sends you by me salutation and friendship.
Restore him the castle which is his inheritance :
His ancestors had it already long in peacefulness ;
But the king of England has disinherited him of it
Wrongly and sinfully, thus he sends you a message by me.
And, if you please, you know that this is the truth.
You were not a child nor of childish age
That you and all the kingdom did not see that.
Now show him love before his baronage :
1400 Surrender him the castle and all the fortress,
And he will give you so much coined money
Never Hubert de Vaus [1] had so much collected.
" Surrender him the castle on such terms,
And become his man on such conditions :
He will give you so much property in fine gold and money,
And much more than we tell you.
" If you do not consent to it to disinherit him,
You must not in any place trust to his person :
He will besiege the castle with his people,
1410 You will not go out of it any day without injury to you ;
And if he can gain the castle by force,
The king of England will be of no avail to you,
Nor all the gold of his kingdom which he could collect,
To prevent you from being drawn on a hurdle and adjudged to
  a bad death."
When lord Robert heard this, he was very calm :
" We do not care about quarrels or threats.
[We are here within good steady people :] [2]

[1] See Dugd. Baron. i. 525.   [2] This line does not occur in the Lincoln MS.

May he be disgraced who will surrender himself as long as victuals
    last !
Tell me, messenger, may God give you honour !
1420 Go to the king of Scotland, who is your lord ;
Say that I inform him I take from him no estate
Nor fees nor inheritance, nor will I ever do so ;
But let him go to king Henry, let him make his complaint
That I hold the castle and tower of Carlisle
By force against him as a true warrior ;
And if my sire the king be angry with me for it,
Let him send me his messenger, but no traitor,
Who may tell me from him : ' Give up this honour
Willingly and cheerfully ; there must be no giving it back
1430 " And if he will not do so, let us make a covenant :
Give me such a respite that I may pass the sea,
And I shall tell my lord, Henry the valiant king,
To give him back his honour as far as he is requiring,
The castle of Carlisle and all belonging to it.
Then he is sure of it, if I have the command for it,
Certainly ; or, if not, were I to die here before,
The castle of my lord I will not surrender to him."
   When the king's messenger the answer had heard,
He said to his companions : " I never saw such thing.
1440 If the king my lord have no pity on him,
I value little all the baronage he has collected here."
And he said to Robert de Vaus : " We will go hence ;
Woe to you that you saw Carlisle as well as king Henry."
Then the messengers departed thence,
And tell their lord all they had heard :
" Sire, king of Scotland, now hear the message.
Robert informs you through me that he fears you not ;
He will not surrender the castle for gold or for silver,
And for Scotland besides, if he had a present of it,
1450 And had rather die before all his people.
There is within the castle enough of wine and corn,
And there is unanimity between him and his people
I must say all that belongs to a messenger.
He does not wish to take from you any thing which is yours ;
But, if he saw his lord to whom the honour belongs,
And he ordered him to leave it by his command,
And only said to him with his own mouth,
' Surrender to king William,' he would do it very readily ;
And he will inform him soon and quickly."
1460 And said king William : " This is a joke of his."
   The king had counsellors, he knew all their business ;
He did not this time any harm to Robert,
But went to Appleby :[1] there he directed his march.
There were no people in it : therefore he took it speedily.
   The king had very soon the castle of Appleby ;
There were no people in it, but it was quite unguarded.

          [1] A town in Westmoreland.

Gospatric [1] the son of Horm, an old grey-headed Englishman,
Was the constable; he soon cried mercy.
 The king had then forgot his sorrow
1470 When he had the castle and the tower of Appleby;
And goes threatening much the king our lord,
Henry the son of Matilda, to whom God give honour!
To vanquish all those may He give him strength and vigour
Who are against him to deprive him of his possessions!
 King William of Scotland has already taken Appleby,
And Roger de Mowbray who was his friend;
And they place within it their serjeants as warders of the marches,
And have appointed three constables in the castle;
They have great joy and laughter enough among themselves:
1480 They think never to lose them till the day of judgment.
They wish to go to Burc; [2] the resolution was soon taken.
If it is not surrendered to them, not a single living being shall go
  out of it;
But the castle was not so unprovided,
That there were not within it more than six knights.
The castle was very soon attacked on all sides;
And the Flemings and the Border-men make a violent assault
  upon them,
And have the first day taken from them the outer fortification,
And soon they left it and placed themselves in the tower.
 Now are they in this tower, they will hold out a short time;
1490 For they set fire to it, they will burn them who are inside it.
[They do not know any plan nor what they can do;
Already the fire is lighted: now they will be burnt here.] [3]
" By my faith! fair sire, if you please, they will not do so;
But will behave like knights: they will stick to the king,
For they see very well they will have no succour."
They cannot hold out longer, they have surrendered to the king.
That is well done which they do now.
They have surrendered to the king, they have great sorrow in their
  hearts.
 But a new knight had come to them that day.
1500 Now hear of his deeds and his great exploits:
When his companions had all surrendered,
He remained in the tower and seized two shields,
He hung them on the battlements, he stayed there long,
And threw at the Scots three sharp javelins;
With each of the javelins he has struck a man dead.
When those failed him, he takes up sharp stakes
And hurled them at the Scots, and confused some of them,
And ever keeps shouting: " You shall all be soon vanquished."
Never by a single vassal was strife better maintained.
1510 When the fire deprived him of the defence of the shields,
He is not to blame if he then surrendered.

[1] See Nicolson and Burn's Hist. of Westmoreland and Cumberland, i. 465.
[2] Brough under Stanemore, in Westmoreland.
[3] These two lines are supplied from the Lincoln MS.

Now is Burc overthrown and the best of the tower.
[Now is Robert de Vaus in some alarm;] [1]
He sends his messenger the same day
To Richard de Luci, who tells him the truth
That Appleby has been taken in the morning,
And the castle of Brough, which is not much worse.
" I have now from no part either aid or succour,
And I think well that the king will give me hard treatment."
20 And Richard de Luci says : " Now let him do the best,
Let him beware of becoming a deceiver for any thing;
But if he loves Henry his good lord,
For him must he endure trouble and grief.
I send him for my part greeting and love;
And news of the king, before fifteen days elapse,
He will have in England, if it pleases God the Saviour."
When Robert heard that, the colour came to his face;
He who before was dejected, now is in joy.
        Of Richard de Luci now hear the truth :
530 By the good sense which he has and his great loyalty,
His lord beyond the sea by his letters he has called ;
The Bishop of Winchester,[2] as it was arranged,
He himself went there through very great friendship,
And said to king Henry : " May God save you !
England salutes you as its defender,
Lord Richard de Luci and all the other baronage
Who adhere to you ; but hear the truth :
They are not ten, so may Lord God help me,
Who adhere to you in right loyalty."
540   Then asks the king : " What then does Richard
De Luci the loyal ? Is he on my side ?"
— " Yes, sire, indeed, he does not do things by halves ;
But would rather let himself be tied to a post with a rope."
    — " And the earl of Arundel, how does he behave ?
Does he side with me ? does he war against us ?"
— " Sire, by my faith ! but he is your well-wisher
In all your need, in the foremost rank."
    — " And Humphrey de Bohun, how has he behaved ?
Against my enemies has he fought ? "
550 — " Sire, by my faith ! I wish to be believed in it :
He is one of the most loyal who has adhered to you."
    — " Near York how behaved the barons ?
And those of Estutevile, do they keep their houses ?"
— " Certainly, sire, if you please, we know it very well,
From those of Estutevile no treasons have come."
    — " And the elected bishop of Lincoln,[3] how is he in the country ?
Can he not fight against his enemies ?"
— " He is, sire, truly your cordial friend ;
He has enough of chevaliers and good border-serjeants."

___

[1] This line occurs only in the Lincoln MS.
[2] This was Richard, surnamed Toclive, or of Ilchester.
[3] Geoffrey, the natural son of Henry II. and Rosamond Clifford.

— " Thomas the son of Bernard and his brother also,
1560 Are they very often with Richard de Luci?"
— " Certainly, sire, if you please, they are very friendly to you,
And Roger le Bigod, who never failed."
— " Now tell me the truth of my land of the north :
Roger d'Estutevile, has he made any agreement?"
— " A thousand men would die there, sire, of bad death
Ere Roger d'Estutevile injure you either right or wrong."
— " Ralph de Glanvile,[1] is he at Richmond,[2]
And lord Robert de Vaus? what are these two barons about?"
1570 Then drew the messenger a profound sigh ;
And the king said to him : " Wherefore are these sighs?
Has then Robert de Vaus committed treason ?
Has he surrendered Carlisle? say nothing but truth."
— " But he keeps it nobly like a gentle baron.
Of his great trouble it is right we should tell you.
The king of Scotland came the other day by Carlisle prancing
And harshly threatening lord Robert de Vaus ;
He asked him for the castle, with this covenant,
That he would give him enough wherewith he should be rich ;
1580 And if he did not do so thenceforth,
He would make them all die of starvation, the little and the great."
— " By my faith," so said the king, " here is a good covenant.
In little time God works, so says the beggar.
What then did the Scot do? did he besiege Carlisle?"
— " By no means, sire, if you please, but he did a more daring thing ;
For he has taken Appleby, for which I very much lament,
And the castle of Brough, I must well acquaint you."
—" How, my good fellow!" said the king, "is then Appleby taken?"
—" Yes, sire, indeed, and all the country :
1590 That has greatly encouraged your mortal enemies.
Some held by you, who have joined them.
Sire, for Robert de Vaus I have been here sent :
Neither wine nor wheat can reach him any longer,
Nor from the side of Richmond will he be assisted more ;
If he has not speedy succour, all will be starved.
Then will Northumberland be completely devastated,
Odinel de Humfranvile at length disinherited ;
Newcastle-on-Tyne will be destroyed,
William de Vesci, his lands and his fees :
1600 The Scots overrun it all like heathen."
— " By God!" so said the king, " it would be a great pity."
Then his eyes shed tears, he sighed deeply :
— " Eh, my good fellow ! what does the bishop of Durham?"
— " He is all one with king William."
— " Saint Thomas," said the king, " preserve me my kingdom ;
I confess myself guilty to you for what others have the blame.
— Fair sir," said the king, " tell me truth,
How do my barons of London my city?"

[1] A memoir of this celebrated baron of the Exchequer may be seen in Dugd.
Baron. i. 423.   [2] A market town in Yorkshire.

— " So may the Lord God help me who remains in Trinity,
1610 They are the most loyal people of all your kingdom.
There is none in the town who is of such an age
As to bear arms, who is not very well armed ;
You would be wrong to think now anything bad of them.
But, sire, now be acquainted with one thing :
Gilbert of Munfichet[1] has fortified his castle,
And says that the men of Clare are allied to him."
— " O God !" so said the king, " now take pity on it,
Preserve my barons of London my city.
    — " Go, lord bishop, into your country.
1620 If God give me health and I may be living,
You will have me at London before fifteen days come,
And I will take vengeance on all my enemies."
He sends for his people, his good worthy serjeants
And earls and barons,—there is not one left out ;
He entrusted Rouen to them, for they are his friends.
The bishop comes back, as I told you just now ;
And Richard de Luci, who never was at a loss,
Has gladly asked news of the king :
" Sir," says the bishop, " he is a worthy king :
1630 He fears not the Flemings the value of a clove of garlick ;
Nor does he, by my faith ! the king of Saint-Denis.
He thinks he shall conquer his enemies so
That you will[2] see him arrive in fifteen days from this."
    Now is Richard de Luci in a great joy ;
He informs Robert de Vaus he would be wrong to be afraid :
He will have succour from the good king his lord
Like loyal knight who has kept his honour.
When Robert heard that above there in that tower,
He never was more delighted at any time.
1640 The king of Scotland came there in the very same day,
And asked for Carlisle, city and tower ;
Or he will have it by force, there will be no retractation.
And Robert de Vaus said : " For God the Creator !
Appoint me a term, and name me a day :
If succour does not come to me from the king my lord,
I will surrender you the castle, and you shall be the commander !"
And king William said : " I have no fear of it ;
You will have no succour, I know well the truth of it."
    Now goes king William straight to Odinel,
1650 He wanted to surprise him to get the castle ;
But the castle was well provided afresh :
Now Odinel will be besieged within there,
For the king of Scotland sends him a challenge.
    Odinel had good people established in the castle :
So he makes defence, never did I see better.
He himself without companions sallied out by force.

---

[1] Dugd. Baron. i. 438.
[2] In MS. Linc. the reading is, "You will see him at London in fifteen days from this."

His people did not wish that he should be there disgraced ;
For they knew very well the king was very bold,
Towards their lord he had a heart swelling and angry ;
1660 And if he could take the castle by [his] gathered host,
He would never have mercy on Odinel in his court.
Odinel departed very sorry from his people,
And they remained within like bold knights.
    Great was the host of Scotland, the noise and the cry.
With Flemings and Border-men the castle was assaulted ;
And those within defended themselves with strength and valour,
For so many wounded outside were knocked down,
They will never see the relations which they had.
And Odinel goes off on his hairy bay horse
1670 To ask for succour that he might be relieved.
    Then Odinel rode so much on the good brown bay,
Day and night always spurring,
That he gathered good valiant people,
Four hundred knights with their shining helmets.
They will be in the battle fighting with him,
They will succour Prudhoe with their trenchant swords.
    Three days lasted the siege, to my knowledge :
Odinel had many good men there within.
Against the Flemings they defend themselves bravely.
1680 They did not lose within, I assure you I tell no lie,
As much as amounted to a silver penny ;
But they lost their fields with all their corn,
And their gardens were ravaged by those bad people ;
And he who could not do more injury, took it into his head
To bark the apple-trees : it was bad vengeance.
    When king William saw that he could not succeed,
Nor take the castle by arrows nor by spears,
He spoke in private to his good counsellor :
    " Let us go to Alnwick, let us leave this one alone.
1690 You will not see with your eyes this first month elapse,
Before Odinel will hold it to his great trouble.
Never will we go from it until we have first had it.
Let us allow our Scots to waste the sea-coast—
Woe to them if they leave standing a house or a church ;
And we will allow the Galloway-men to go in another direction,
To kill the men in Odinel's land :
We will go to Alnwick to besiege the castle,
And both our hosts shall come to help our Frenchmen ;
But they will have first made so great a disturbance,
1700 That this country will be destroyed. Now let us think of hast-
        ening."
    It was on Thursday evening that the king spoke,
And Frenchmen and Flemings agreed to his words.
Friday in the morning his trumpet was sounded :
This great host departed and his fierce baronage,
And come to Alnwick ; they did not delay longer ;
But the Scots burnt and wasted the country.

The church of Saint-Laurence [1] was that day violated,
Three priests in the church were by force castrated,
And three hundred men murdered, without a word of falsehood;
1710 Never will they see a relation or any of their kindred.
And Odinel de Umfranvile has so well managed,
Such succour has gained, so help me Lord God,
That the king of Scotland will be enraged at heart;
No relation that he had was ever so disgraced.
The king was at Alnwick with his great gathered host;
And Odinel rides with the fierce company,
William [2] d'Estutevile who helps him very much,
And Ralph de Glanvile is not backward,
Lord Bernard de Baliol [3] with his furbished sword
1720 Will lay hard upon the people of Albany,
And William de Vesci do not forget there.
The archbishop of York [4] gave them lodgings,
And sixty knights of his chivalry.
To Newcastle-on-Tyne, when the night is advanced,
Is come Odinel, who conducts and guides them:
That is the truth, whatever anybody may say about it.
There they heard news of this king of Albany,
That he was at Alnwick with a small suit.
With the Flemings and Frenchmen the Scots were not,
1730 But burn the country each of them at his best.
If it pleased you to hear a good deed done by good people,
I will tell you of this, of my own knowledge.
They have consulted together what they should do and how,
If they should go and attack this king and his people.
Thus answers Odinel: " Shame to him that forbids it!
I will strike there, please God, all at first:
He has done me a very great harm, and my heart is grieved at it;
And if God allowed us to take vengeance,
We shall make a good job of it, by my knowledge.
1740 Let us go and attack them; and, if he waits for us,
He will be discomfited, and his host likewise."
Said Bernard de Baliol: " He who has no courage now
Can have no honour nor anything which appertains to it."
Said Ralph de Glanvile: " Let us act prudently:
Let us send a spy to reckon their forces;
And we will come afterwards, if God allows us.
Since the Scots are not there, we do not care the least about them,"
Odinel sends for all his best troops,
Roger the son of Richard has also sent for his.
1750 Now have the barons each assumed courage,
And go to Alnwick by night closely.
And then in the morning, when the day dawned,
The king of Scotland had his head well armed

---

[1] This is the church of Warkworth. See line 1903.
[2] According to Dugdale (Baron. i. 455), the name of the baron who captured William was Robert, and not William.
[3] See the authority last cited, i. 523.
[4] Archbishop Roger, consecrated A.D. 1154, died 1181.

And five hundred knights in a band,
Who all keep saying to him : " Beware of trust to cowardice.
Yours is Northumberland, whether they weep or laugh."
    And said the king of Scotland : " We will wait for our host,
And then with great vigour we shall assault the castle.
Because of the heat, which is great, lords, let us dine."
1760 And he uncovers his head, very well we know it :
We who compose this history do not wish to lie.
    Before the castle the king had stopped ;
His servants bring him what he has dined upon.
And our knights went into a copse ;
There they have their spy who told them all.
Says Ralph de Glanvile : " Thank the Lord God !
Now take your arms, beware of being fearful."
Then might you see knights quickly stirring,
Mounting on their horses and their arms seizing ;
1770 There will be no impediment to keep them from attacking them :
That which one of them wishes, pleases the other.
    The king of Scotland was brave, wonderful and bold,
Before Alnwick he stood unarmed.
I do not relate a fable as one who has heard say,
But as one who was there, and I myself saw it.
When these had once cried the war-signal of Vesci
And " Glanvile, knights !" and " Baliol !" likewise,
Odinel de Humfreville raised a cry of his own,
And another that of Estuteville, a bold knight.
1780 Then knew king William that he was nearly betrayed ;
Quickly he stirred himself, he was not disconcerted.
    The king arms himself soon and hastily,
And mounted on a horse which was not slow,
And goes to the fight with very great boldness.
The first whom he struck, he knocks to the ground.
The fight was very great of the king and his troops.
Every thing would have gone on well, to my knowledge,
Were it not for a serjeant who rushes up to him ;
With the lance which he held, he pierces his horse.
1790 You must not ask if the king was sorrowful :
The sin of the Scots is an encumbrance to him.
The king falls to the ground, and the grey horse.
    The king and his horse are both on the ground,
He could not get up, the horse lay upon him :
Now he has enough of labour and trouble and vexations,
When servants and esquires pass by him ;
He will hear news, to my knowledge, to-day ;
He cannot much help himself nor others.
    Great was the battle and stubborn on both sides ;
1800 You might see darts enough thrown and arrows shot,
The bold fighting and the cowardly flying.
Of the unfortunate Flemings great carnage was made,
[You might see] their bowels dragged from the bodies through the
    fields ;

Never again in their country will they cry, Arras !
The king lay on the ground thrown down, as I tell you ;
Between his legs lay the horse upon him ;
Never again will he rise from it for relation or friend,
If the horse is not drawn from him, with which he is encumbered ;
He will always be humbled and disgraced.
1810 He was soon taken, with my two eyes I saw it,
By Ralph de Glanvile, to whom he then surrendered ;
And all his boldest knights are taken.
There was no favour : all were enemies.
Our knights on this side, never did I see better,
Love not the Flemings, who had then betrayed them ;
But they keep killing them.   I know not what more to say to you.
The king surrenders himself prisoner to Ralph, truly ;
He could not do otherwise, what else could he do ?
And Ralph was glad, when he sees and hears
1820 That the war of the king is really finished.
England is at peace, and the good people
Will no longer dread the Scots : they will not injure them at all.
Ralph de Glanvile has the king in custody,
[And he surrendered to him, and he grants it readily ;
He was not so delighted in any day of his life.][1]
He takes off his armour, and forgets nothing.
On a palfrey mounted this king of Albany ;
So they led him gently, whatever may be said to you.
At Newcastle-on-Tyne they take lodgings,
1830 And the others remained for their knights-service
And take those knights towards Albany.
Now the battle on both sides was well fought.
Certainly, our royal knights behave very well,
And those of Albany were very good vassals ;
But when they had lost what they regarded most,
Their natural lord, who was brought by them,
These are not all loyal to their king,
And they are knocked to the ground from their horses ;
In the midst of the battle they will be taken one and all.
1840 It is no wonder if the gay and the cheerful are sorrowful.
Lord Roger de Mowbray went away flying ;
He behaved courteously, what should he wait for ?
All are his enemies, who are there fighting ;
And if they can take him, there will be no safeguard
From the king of England executing his pleasure on him.
And lord Adam de Porz, a very valiant baron,
Went away with him.   Now they go spurring on.
It was well for them, God is a great guard to them,
For they were not caught by any man alive.
1850 Certainly, if Adam de Porz had not been so far advanced,
He would have lost that day the little and the great ;
But God did not consent to it, who is a powerful King :
It would have been too great damage, for he is very valiant.

[1] These two lines occur only in the Lincoln MS.

Now I will tell you who were fighting well
Before Alnwick, the castle of which I sing :
Lord Alan de Lanceles, as long as he was standing,
Defended himself on the grey war-horse.
He was very old, a very great knight,
He had not jousted full thirty years before ;
1860 But was a good knight and of great knowledge.
If the king had known it, his word would have been welcome
Lord Alan was then taken and kept ;
Now he must give ransom, for his property is great.
    William de Mortimer [1] behaved very well that day
He goes among the ranks like a mad boar,
Gives great blows and often takes his share of them ;
He found opposed to him a true knight,
Lord Bernard de Baliol, of whom you hear me speak ;
He knocked down him and his charger,
1870 He put him on parole, as is done for a knight.
Lord Bernard does well, he is not to be blamed ;
At the end of the battle he will be praised
Who strikes best with sword and best fights.
Raoul le Rus behaved well, but could not hold long :
More than one hundred attacked him, so as to impede him com-
      pletely.
If then he surrendered, it is no wonder ;
Unhappy man to have seen this war : he will pay very dear for it.
    Certainly Richard Maluvel behaved himself gloriously,
He gave enough of great blows, and he takes enough,
1880 As long as he was on horseback he feared nothing ;
He had a very good horse, good are his equipments,
And himself bold and brave, so I say without any falsehood.
He did on that day, to my knowledge,
As much as thirteen followers then present with him ;
But he loses the war-horse : for which he is very sorry.
It is struck through, and falls immediately :
It is a great pity, for he will be very sorry for it.
And over lord Richard stood many people ;
There was none that did not say : " Surrender directly."
1890 He therefore surrendered himself with very great unwillingness ;
Woe to him that he saw king William and his wild rashness.
I cannot tell you, it would be too long,
All those who were taken and led away with sorrow ;
But I will count to you nearly a hundred,
Whom William de Vesci ransomed quite at his pleasure.
And Bernard de Baliol and the other good people,
Walter de Bolebec,[2] Odinel likewise,
Had prisoners at their departure.
    Lords, do not marvel if they are discomfited :
1900 The Scots have this day more than a thousand badly wounded,
And death has parted the sons from their fathers.

    [1] He was one of the hostages for the king of Scotland at the treaty of Falaise.
    [2] See Dugd. Baron. i. 452. The Lincoln MS. incorrectly reads " Holebec."

One might see the grief, the tears and the cries
Which these wretches make in the monastery of Saint-Laurence; [1]
Some have their bodies and breasts cut open.
The shorn priests were not spared there :
There is no occasion to ask if God is provoked at it
And if He detested king William for it ;
For his sin are many severely wounded,
And he himself was there on that day discomfited.

1910   As far as I know, now hear the truth :
The king of England had then arrived,
And in the morning was then reconciled to saint Thomas.
When the king of the Scots was taken and brought,
At Newcastle-on-Tyne he was lodged at night,
And Ralph de Glanvile conducted him from thence.
Now he comes to Richmond, where he must sojourn
Until king Henry shall make known his pleasure.
  The king was truly at saint Thomas the martyr's,
Where he confessed himself guilty, sinful and repentant,

1920 And took his penance, do not consider it a light one ;
He took leave of it, he would not stay there ;
He wished to go to London, where he had great desire to go,
To see his city and his good people.
For the war of Scotland they have sorrowful hearts,
They feared much the king, and he is very sorry for it ;
But he will soon hear quite differently,
That all his enemies have taken flight.
  When they heard news of the king at London,
Each equipped himself richly for his own part;

1930 In rich stuffs of silk they were variously dressed,
There is none that has not an ambling palfrey ;
And they issue from the town in a marvellous procession.
He ought to be a king truly who has such people under him.
  Certainly, lord Henry le Blunt was the very first
Who went forward to kiss his lord.
You might easily have gone a league of land,
So long did the embracing of the king and his barons last ;
And the king of England begins to thank them :
They are very loyal subjects, so he says to them at first ;

1940 And they thank him as their liege lord.
" Sire," so said Gervase Suplest, " let it be.
Let it not please the Lord God who made land and sea
That any one should call the Londoners traitors !
They would not commit treason if their limbs were cut off."
— " Certainly," so says the king, " they may boast
And I will requite them, if they have need of me."
Thus they accompany the king to Westminster.
  The Londoners rejoice at the arrival of their lord,
They give him presents and they pay him great honour ;

1950 But he was pensive and somewhat distracted
For the king of Scotland who was raging,

[1] See line 1707.

And Roger de Mowbray, a noble warrior,
Who were destroying his land by night and by day.
But before the right hour of sleeping came,
There reached him such news as gave him great honour.
    The king had gone into his own private room
When the messenger came; he had undergone much fatigue:
He had neither drunk nor eaten three days of the week,
Nor closed his eyes on account of the certain news;
1960 But day and night he wearies himself in travelling:
He did very wisely, he will have a handsome present.
    The king was leaning on his elbow and sleeping a little,
A servant was at his feet who rubbed them gently;
There was no noise nor cry, and nobody spoke there,
No harp nor violin was heard there at all,
When the messenger came to the door and softly called.
And says the chamberlain: "Who are you there?"
— "A messenger am I, friend; now come nearer.
Lord Ralph de Glanvile sent me here
1970 To speak with the king, for he has great need of it."
    And said the chamberlain: "In the morning let it be done."
— "By my faith!" said the messenger, "but I must speak to him
      instantly.
My lord has in his heart grief and vexation:
So allow me to enter, kind chamberlain."
And says the chamberlain: "I dare not do it.
The king is asleep: you must withdraw."
While thus they speak the king awoke,
And heard a crying at the door: "Open! open!"
— "Who is there?" said the king; "you must tell me."
1980 — "Sire," said the chamberlain, "you shall know it directly.
It is a messenger from the north, you know him very well:
A man of Ralph de Glanvile's; Brien is his name."
— "By my faith!" said the king, "now I am very sorrowful:
He wants help, let him come in."
The messenger entered, who was very well bred
And saluted the king, as you may soon hear:
" Sire king, may God save you, who dwells in Trinity,
Your own person first, and then all your private friends!"
— "Brien," said the king, "what news do you bring?
1990 Has the king of Scotland entered Richmond?
Is Newcastle-on-Tyne, the fortress, seized?
Is Odinel de Umfranvile taken or driven out?
And are all my barons ejected from their lands?
Messenger, by thy faith, tell me the truth.
They have served me unfortunately, if they be not revenged."
— "Sire," so said the messenger, "hear me a little.
Your barons of the north are good folks enough.
On behalf of my lord hear me graciously.
He sends you by me greeting and friendship,
2000 And my lady much more, with whom you are well acquainted.
[He informs you by me there is no need of your stirring.

The king of Scotland is taken and all his baronage."][1]
And says king Henry : " Do you speak the truth ?"
— " Yes, sire, indeed, you will know it in the morning :
[The archbishop of York, a wise and learned man,][2]
Will send you two private messengers ;
But I hastened first, who knew the truth.
I have scarcely slept these four last days,
Neither eaten nor drunk, so I am very hungry ;
2010 But, at your pleasure, give me a recompense for it."
And answered the king : " You would be wrong to doubt it.
If you have told me the truth, you are rich enough.
Is the king of Scotland taken ? tell me the truth."
— " Yes, sire, by my faith ! May I be nailed to a cross,
Or hanged by a rope, or burnt at a great stake,
If to-morrow, ere noon, it be not all confirmed !"
— " Then," says king Henry, " God be thanked for it,
And saint Thomas the martyr and all the saints of God !"
Then the messenger went to his inn,
2020 He has great plenty to eat and drink ;
And the king is so glad in the night and so delighted
That he went to the knights and awoke them all :
" Barons, awake, it is a good night for you.
I have heard such a thing as will make you glad :
The king of Scotland is taken, so I have been told for truth.
Just now the news came to me when I ought to have been in bed."
And say the knights : " Now thanks be to the Lord God ;
Now the war is finished, and your realm in peace."
 Very fine seemed this night to king Henry.
2030 Next day, before noon, news came to him
From the archbishop of York whom they call Roger,
Who salutes his lord who leads the loyal.
When the king sees the messengers, never was he more glad ;
And sees that they say the same thing, so he answered them :
" Last night I heard the news when I was much displeased ;
To him who brought it me, reward shall be given."
He seized a switch, and handed it to Brien,
Ten liveries of his land for the trouble he had.
Hastily he takes his messengers, and sent them to David
2040 Who was brother of the king of Scotland ; never did I see a better
  man.
He was at Leicester as vassal brave and bold ;
But he never was so sorrowful, as when he heard that message.
The king of England informs him the circumstances are such,
There is nothing but to surrender and to ask for his mercy.
David knew not in all the world better advice,
But to surrender the castle and then to come to king Henry.
Lords, all this business was done thus in eight days :
The king of England has peace, all his enemies are taken.
 Now he orders the king of Scotland to be led to him quickly ;

---

[1] These two lines occur only in the Lincoln MS., instead of the two preceding ones.   [2] Omitted in the Lincoln MS.

2050 For news came to him, that he must cross the sea :
His city Rouen is besieged ; he would not stay longer.
He takes David away with him, and goes to the sea ;
And Brien returned, who has no mind to stay ;
And he said to his lord that he must immediately bring
The king of Scotland to Southampton : the king desires he should
    pass the sea.
Henry the king, the son of Matilda, in a lucky hour may he have
    been born !
He waits at Southampton for wind and weather and a good breeze;
And lord Ralph de Glanvile makes haste to travel,
He brings with him the king of Scotland, who has a very sorrowful
    heart.
2060   Ralph de Glanvile and the king of Albany
Hasten to reach the king and his fleet.
The king had a good breeze, so he did not wait for them ;
When they came to Southampton, he was in Normandy.
I will tell you the truth, whatever any body may tell you.
The king had commanded on limb and life
Ralph de Glanvile, who had him in custody,
That he should cross in haste, and should not tarry.
The king arrived at Rouen, when the dawn appeared.
Before the evening came, peace was established ;
2070 And the king came to France with his great gathered host
And he has gone to France.   The war is now finished.

END OF THE CHRONICLE.

Also publised by
LLANERCH

THE MYSTICAL WAY
AND THE ARTHURIAN QUEST
Derek Bryce
ISBN 0947992073

ARTHUR AND THE BRITONS
IN HISTORY AND ANCIENT POETRY
W. F. Skene
ISBN 0947992111

CELTIC FOLK-TALES
FROM ARMORICA
F. M. Luzel
ISBN 0947992049

THE CELTIC LEGEND
OF THE BEYOND
Anatole Le Braz
ISBN 0947992065

THE LEGENDARY XII HIDES
OF GLASTONBURY
Ray Gibbs
ISBN 0947992154

From booksellers,
or direct mail-order;
write for a current list to
Llanerch Enterprises,
Felinfach, Lampeter,
Dyfed, Wales.
SA48 8PJ.